FASTER
AS A
MASTER

BREAKING DOWN BARRIERS, JOURNEYING TOWARD WHOLENESS

Bruce W. Conner

Text and photographs © 2014 by Bruce W. Conner

All rights reserved. Published 2014. No part of this book may be reproduced in any manner whatsoever without written permission from the publisher, except in the case of brief quotations embodied in critical articles and reviews.

Bruce W. Conner

http://www.brucewconner.com

Design by Robert Caron, Northbrook IL

Printed in the United States

ISBN 978-0-9907536-2-9

DEDICATION

To Maripat, the love of my life, with whom
I share this fantastic journey.

ACKNOWLEDGEMENTS

To GOD for his infinite love and wisdom; the love of my life, partner, and wife, Maripat, without whose love and support this book and life would not be possible; our four children Bradley, Jamie, James, Patrick; my granddaughters Gracie and Violet—you are my inspiration and motivation to be the best I can be; to my parents Harold and Jackie Conner for their undying love and support; my brothers, Bart and Mike, for being the best brothers, friends, confidants, and partners in crime; coaches Dave Cruikshank and Nancy Swider-Peltz, Sr. for their expertise and friendship; The guys I hang out with—Vince O'Brien, Carl Alguire, Bryan Forrestal, Vic Pfammatter, Dave Baranowski, Steve Heaviland, my closest friends that trudge this happy road with me; my medical support team, Dr. Joe Meis, Dr. Randy Horning, and Joe Mitchell for their knowledge and wisdom; my skating family and tribe of skaters with whom I share the ice—Jeffrey Gingold, Marv and Kathy Hughes, Olu Sijuwade, Andrew Love, and all the other training partners over the years, young and old; to all the outstanding aviation professionals I have worked with over the years, pilots, flight attendants, dispatchers, and mechanics; to my oldest friend Bruce Bondy—without his help and encouragement this book would not have the form it does today; to my editor Ruth Hull Chatlien, I am in deep gratitude for your help in all phases of writing this book and the way you treated me as an athlete as I "trained" my writing skills for the final form of this manuscript; to my book designer Robert Caron for your help in getting this book to its final print and electronic form.

INTRODUCTION

When I think about my brother, Bruce Conner, this famous quote comes to mind:

"The credit belongs to the man who is actually in the arena, whose face is marred by dust and sweat and blood; who strives valiantly; who errs, who comes short again and again, because there is no effort without error and shortcoming; but who does actually strive to do the deeds; who knows great enthusiasms, the great devotions; who spends himself in a worthy cause; who at the best knows in the end the triumph of high achievement, and who at the worst, if he fails, at least fails while daring greatly, so that his place shall never be with those cold and timid souls who neither know victory nor defeat."

—Theodore Roosevelt

Bruce Conner defines what it is to be a <u>true</u> champion. He has discovered what makes his heart sing, but most importantly he has the courage and discipline to go for it.

Bruce Conner's success in speed skating, and in life for that matter, is not just about his master's world records and titles. His accomplishments inspire us to re-think our own lives. How many of us can actually say that we found that "sweet spot" in life where you can actually tap into the incredible energy, beauty, inspiration, and grace that surrounds us?

When you follow Bruce's honest and heartfelt journey, you may find yourself asking the same questions about what is the true meaning of success.

It is relatively easy to set a bold goal. However, it is something else altogether to build a plan, follow through, and execute that goal. Bruce's story is not just a success story, but more importantly, it is a story about striving for "significance." By setting daring goals, Bruce demonstrates the enormous courage it takes to expose his dreams and desires as well as his vulnerabilities as an athlete and as a human being.

Who among us has the courage to do that on a world stage? Bruce Conner does!

I admire my brother Bruce Conner, and I think you will too.

Bart Conner

1984 Olympic Gold Medalist

FORWARD

by Jeffrey Gingold

He may not have planned it this way, but the 500-meter speed skating race is emblematic of Bruce Conner's life. It is a unique distance to race because when he cuts his blades into the ice at the start line, Bruce can see the finish line 100 meters ahead him. But simply passing it the first time is not the end point since the race requires the skater to loop the ice oval before sprinting to the finish. While the finish is out of immediate reach, clearly seeing a path to the goal ahead of you is the culmination of tactical preparation to vault beyond the lines. Without it, merely showing up on the race day won't work.

In this insightful book, Bruce Conner shares how being engaged in life at age 50 led him to discover hidden goals and the means to achieve them. The discussion is honest, and his goals are bold, demonstrating how some personal walls are best taken down one brick at a time.

Whether training to qualify for the Olympics or as a commercial airline pilot, Bruce reveals how his competitive edge is guided by a detailed and profound sense of actions to prepare his mind, body, and spirit to overcome perceived limits. He details how to break down seemingly impassable barriers by dismantling any challenges. Bruce loves to teach what he has learned, and even if you do not intend on approaching an Olympic level of performance, there is much to gain from his personal elite training methods. Build a plan for yourself with a purposeful network and surpass previously set aspirations.

See yourself on the ice and in his blades, and learn to ask yourself the right questions about training, life networks, and how to adjust when faced with adversity. After Bruce reached the age of 50, he focused his path through acknowledging his barriers, whether from others, nature, or self-imposed, allowing himself to surpass discouragement. His passion for disciplined techniques led him to discover how to excel faster than competitors half his age. Race numbers are the proof of his tactics. Get behind Bruce to feel the pull of his racing draft and learn for yourself how to how to erase your own limitations.

While shattering personal barriers to success, Bruce Conner demonstrates that perhaps the greatest victory is beyond the podium. By openly assessing personal hurdles, you can begin to intentionally dismantle the temporary obstacles and vault forward. Whether flying with Bruce on ice or across the sky, learn how to re-assess and exceed your own expectations. Flatten the walls that limit you, find "boots" that fit, sharpen your blades, and choose a faster lane that leads to your goals. Go to the start, ready, go.

Jeffrey N. Gingold is a fellow speed skater and the internationally acclaimed author of the award-winning book, Facing the Cognitive Challenges of Multiple Sclerosis, *2nd Edition, and* Mental Sharpening Stones.

CONTENTS

Dedication iii
Acknowledgements iv
Introduction v
Forward vii
Prologue 11

PART ONE

Chapter 1 A Chance Meeting 18
Chapter 2 Am I Good Enough? 23
Chapter 3 A Pilgrimage and Healing Old Wounds . . . 37
Chapter 4 The Love of a Father 50
Chapter 5 Asking for What I Need from the Universe . . 55

PART TWO

Chapter 6 Breaking Down Barriers I:
           An Example from Skating 64
Chapter 7 Breaking Down Barriers II:
           An Example from Piloting 71
Chapter 8 How to Break Down Limiting Beliefs and
           Other Barriers 80
Chapter 9 My Final Speed Skating Barrier 87

PART THREE

Chapter 10 Building Networks for Support I:
Parents and Grandparents. 98

Chapter 11 Building Networks for Support II:
Childhood and Adolescence 106

Chapter 12 Building Networks for Support III: Adult . . 113

Chapter 13 Goals 120

Chapter 14 Ego and Emotion 133

Chapter 15 The "A" game 140

Chapter 16 Nutrition 149

Chapter 17 Coaching and the Coach-Athlete
Relationship 154

Chapter 18 Training I: General Training Principles . . . 161

Chapter 19 Training II: Injuries and Prevention 174

Chapter 20 Training III: Reevaluating the Plan. 179

Chapter 21 Competition 191

Chapter 22 Balance and Priorities 197

Chapter 23 Mental Support. 201

Chapter 24 Courage 206

Record Times. 212

APPENDIX

Chapter Wisdom Recap 216

Thoughts on Sochi 2014 Winter Olympic Games 218

Bibliography for Further Reading. 221

PROLOGUE

We all want to be great. As I get older, I want to be great again. Happy, loved, healthy—those are the qualities I aspire to be. To be whole in body, mind, and spirit is the reward. We are more capable of attaining those things than we give ourselves credit for.

Qualifying for the U.S. Olympic long track speed skating trials for the Torino 2006 Olympics at the age of 49 was going to be one of the hardest and most challenging things I had ever done in my life. This challenge would push me to be at my best physically, mentally, emotionally, and spiritually. It would also be one of the most rewarding things I had ever done. I would have to skate significantly faster than I did when I was a teenager on the U.S. national team from 1974 through 1976. I would have to go faster than any man of my age had ever gone.

The drive to qualify started when I was a teenager on the U.S. National team in 1974. My parents' philosophy about raising three boys was to keep us tired by channeling our energy through the outlet of sports. As a result, my two brothers and I all achieved a great deal. I am the oldest, Bart is next by two years, and Mike is the youngest, following Bart by three years. When I was about 14, it became evident that Bart was better at his sport, gymnastics, than Mike and I were at speed skating. I remember a couple of times I was asked to be nice to Bart when he had an upcoming competition. Even though my parents never specifically verbalized that Bart's career was a priority, I felt that the focus shifted towards Bart. As the oldest son and a natural leader, I accepted that role. During this time I lost my voice. This created a disconnect in me and a wound that would not heal, just scab over.

In my adult life, I woke up to a 25-year marriage in which I had also lost my voice. I poured all I had into building my career and family life. Athletic passion was diverted to my passion for flying and family.

PROLOUGE

The energy I spent on my marriage was wasted, especially at the end. The death of my marriage and the subsequent struggle for my identity was frightening. Who was I? Who had I become? Where did I want to go, and what did I want to do and be? All these essential questions needed answers. In due time, I would be able to address them all and be whole as never before. Front and center, my skating was something tangible to work on and a distinct way out of my predicament. Could speeding around a track become the metaphor for my life? By answering yes, I had a vehicle for my path forward.

Competing as a youngster from age 12 till 19, I achieved a great deal during the 1960s and 1970s. After I won a few competitions as a long track ice speed skater, I was on the U.S. national team from 1974 through 1976. My younger brother Bart made three Olympic teams: 1976, 1980, and 1984. Bart is a two-time Olympic gymnastics champion. My youngest brother Mike won the first national medal in our family in short track speed skating when he was 13. I am very proud of my brothers and their accomplishments, as they are of mine.

When I did not make the Olympic team in 1976, I was devastated. I worked harder than anyone, so I believed I deserved to be on that team that went to Innsbruck, Austria. Years later, I can now look back and see that I trained myself into the ground. Athletes call it overtraining.

Discouraged by the failure, I amputated that part of my life for more than 20 years. As a much older and hopefully wiser adult, I returned to the sport that I loved. Opening up old wounds from my past was an inevitable result of that decision. Fear had held me back for decades. Was I ready to deal with the memory of my past? I had to find out, or those very deep wounds would never completely heal and I would never be quite whole. Cautious about the pitfalls of my past, treading lightly as I returned, I decided that making the same mistakes was not an option. Time heals wounds, but it also hardens scabs. My fear of more suffering was very real. Pulling off the scab was going to hurt. Healing from the inside, from down deep, was the only answer. The core of my being was screaming for help.

My mother had died from cancer in April of 2000, and I was still having a tough time accepting it and needing relief. I went through the five stages of grieving for her death as well as many other hurts in my life. Doing the work to heal from the inside was my task. Forcing my pain below the surface was not possible anymore; I had to face it. Going back to the old way of thinking was not an option. I was striving for answers, from my youth, from midlife, from a broken marriage. How could I move forward?

I was not sure what was around the corner, but I was willing to address my humanness because I knew my very survival was at stake. By returning to speed skating, the sport that had brought me so much pleasure and anguish, I would ultimately be journeying toward wholeness.

My need to achieve was born in a very fertile environment, a combination of wanting approval from my parents and contending with sibling rivalry. I am very competitive, so I wondered if my struggle was about the external achievement or self-acceptance? My survival depended on what I was about to discover.

Since I finally felt ready to tackle my past, the time was right to do this work and start healing. The tangible evidence of my extraordinary achievement in speed skating is visible. What is unseen—and more important—is the internal work of healing the wounds of my past.

Sport is one of the ways that I connect in a tangible, measurable way to my own inward journey of self-exploration. Going after what creates meaning in my life and trusting that I can handle the stress that follows sets me up for a journey to wholeness. Any activity, external or internal, can become the vehicle for this important journey. The principles are universal. I hope that this book can help you find your path to breaking down self-limiting beliefs and achieving healing.

Let me give another example. Another passion of mine is flying airplanes. An eye doctor told me when I received my first pair of glasses at age 16 that I would never fly airplanes for a living. It was widely believed then that you needed perfect vision and military training to become an airline pilot. Despite those warnings, I am now at the top of

PROLOUGE

my field as a United Boeing-747 captain. By not accepting the idea that my less-than-perfect vision was an insurmountable barrier, I broke it down before it could become a reality for me.

When I was young and began skating, I could not imagine how rich my life would become because of this sport. Now, as a master's athlete, I have reconnected with my passion for skating, training, goals, and achievement.

I am part of an incredible, growing masters sports movement (sports for athletes over 30). In speed skating, we have an international as well as national governing bodies that oversee the rules and sanction masters' competitions. Age groups start at 30 with 5-year increments ending in the 85+ category for men and 75+ women. Masters-only races can be found many times each year around the globe, including a yearly World All-Around and Sprint Championships.

Skating has come full circle for me. Through my sport, I have learned much about myself; skating exposes me like no other sport. If my body is not responding the way I expect, there is always a deeper reason. It is up to me to find its cause and a way to correct it. If I am off balance physically, mentally, emotionally, or spiritually, the ice and my competitors will give me immediate feedback. It is up to me then to regain and maintain my balance to move forward in skating—and in my life. Skating is a mirror for how to live my life, to learn, change, and grow.

I like to do things that are challenging and thus rewarding. With the imagination to dream it, the insight to break down my limiting beliefs, and the willingness to do the work, I can achieve almost anything!

To break through barriers and to change my life, I must change my thinking. Every action starts with a thought.

Here is one of my favorite quotations that reflects my philosophy:

"We are what we repeatedly do; excellence then is not an act but a habit."

—Aristotle

This is what I believe and what I strive for on my current path.

I have divided this book into three sections. The first tells parts of my story and thereby builds a case for what I have done. The second deals with my philosophy of breaking down barriers and the beliefs that limit us. The third details all the tools I have used in my life to facilitate and enhance my journey.

I hope you will be inspired to successful living and a journey toward wholeness.

PROLOUGE

PART ONE

PART ONE

CHAPTER 1

A CHANCE MEETING

As a United Airlines first officer on the Boeing 727, I was on reserve in January 1988. This means being available to fly on a short notice. The United crew desk called and assigned me a trip that would end up in Calgary, Alberta, Canada, at about noon. It was one month before the 1988 Olympic Games. Calgary built the first-ever indoor 400-meter oval in the world for the Games. I was intrigued by the idea of skating indoors on a track that long and wondered if I could have the opportunity to try it, even though I had been retired from the sport for more than twelve years. Excited at the prospect of getting back on the ice again, I sharpened my skates from 1975 and packed them along with my old one-piece racing suit to take to Calgary.

Traditionally, in the Chicago area, we skaters started our season in September on an indoor hockey rink, skating what is now called short track. As soon as the weather supported outdoor ice, we transitioned to outdoor long track skating. We skated as long as possible outdoors, usually from early December through February. Park districts would flood open fields and maintain them as long as it was cold enough to keep ice. Sometimes frozen lakes were used for practice and racing. The only nearby outdoor 400-meter rink that had artificial refrigeration coils under the ice to keep it cool and open longer was at the Wisconsin state fairgrounds in West Allis, a western suburb of Milwaukee. My true passion, when it comes to skating, is on a 400-meter oval, racing time trials. The rink in Wisconsin was subject to the current weather conditions. The wind, cold, and snow were always a challenge.

The prospect of skating indoors on a 400-meter oval was "out of this world" for me. After arriving in downtown Calgary, I broke out my newly sharpened skates and took a short commuter train ride to the University of Calgary where the rink was. When I asked to skate, the receptionist said the rink was closed to the public for the month before the Games. She told me that the national teams were in town training. The U.S. team was already there, and the Germans would arrive later that day. The Americans would show up in about an hour, so I went to lunch and came back hoping to run into some of my old friends who were still skating. An hour later, just as I was walking into the lobby of the oval, Nancy Swider-Peltz, Sr. was walking out. Nancy and I have known each other since we started racing when we were both 12 years old. She had just made her fourth Olympic team and was carrying her one-year-old daughter Nancy Jr. in her arms through the rink lobby.

Nancy was very surprised to see me since I had not been around the sport since 1975. She asked why I was there. I explained that I was on a trip, had brought my skates, and was interested in skating. Nancy said that since I was a former national team member, I could join them and would be welcome to skate. I was so happy. I had not put my skates on since the trials in December 1975. I was a little nervous but very interested in the new indoor ice. I was not disappointed.

After lacing up my skates, I set out to explore what was once familiar territory. Surprised at how much my body remembered from so long ago, I concluded that muscle memory is amazing. The ice was as smooth as could be, and the air was about 60 degrees F. I could have skated in short sleeves. Although indoor tracks have no wind, in fact, as the skaters went around in packs, they stirred up a continuous tailwind. It was paradise. Because it is maintained to have consistent conditions, the indoor stadium took out all the weather and ice variables. Even though this is a winter sport, my body functions better when I am not freezing. Going 35 miles per hour in 60-degree air feels like about 40 degrees.

The defensive wall that I had built to separate me from skating after amputating that part of my life at age 19 began to crack, and a bright light started shining through that opening. I felt the pull of skating very strongly and started to remember the good parts and not the emotional scars of 1975. The smell of the ice and the familiar skaters' physiques were two great sensory clues to the world I had walked away from. The feel of the leather skate boot and attached blade on the near

PART ONE

perfect ice was summoning me to push, to glide, and to push again. Soon I was feeling the familiar strain on the legs, heart, and lungs. Nearly silent gliding of the blade on the ice accompanied the wind rushing by my ears. Speed on ice is the ultimate payoff. Leaning into the turns felt familiar again. I experienced a feeling of oneness with the ice, the speed, the wind. This time and place held a rightness for me that was hard to explain at the moment. I knew I was born to skate, and being back on the ice confirmed that. To push hard into the ice and generate speed is exhilarating. Physically demanding, mentally challenging, emotionally taxing, and spiritually rewarding is the essence of pure skating. There is grace when the outer world of skating meets the inner world. Any day I can skate is a great day because it feeds my soul.

I was on the ice for about an hour, skating only short distances of a lap or two at a time, gliding in between efforts while watching the other skaters training hard for the upcoming Olympics. I thanked Nancy for her help in getting back on the ice because, if indoor ice and perfect conditions were what the future of skating was going to be like, then I had to figure out a way to get back to this sport that I had forgotten I loved so much. I was ready to start tearing down the barrier that separated me from the emotional pain. Doing so would hopefully open up a new world of skating.

Trusting I would be led in the right direction, I left the rink in awe. The next month, I watched the 1988 Olympic Games with a special eye on the skating. All the world records fell in this competition. Skaters were going faster than ever in history because of the indoor conditions, the great ice, the longer season. The 3,650-foot elevation above sea level in Calgary also helped cut down the aerodynamic drag. A new day was dawning in speed skating with this indoor oval, and I wanted to be part of it. Somehow, I would figure out a way to make it happen. I knew I would have to be patient because I had a young family and career to think about, but the seeds had been sown for me to come back to the sport I loved. I would let them germinate for as long as it took.

In 1993, the rink that I grew up skating on in Milwaukee was rebuilt on the same spot and made into an indoor facility. Here was my chance. I had two children: my son Bradley born in 1985 and my daughter Jamie born in 1991. When Jamie entered school full time in 1997, I started skating about once a week or so. Driving 150 miles round trip to the only (at that time) indoor 400-meter oval in the country was hard, but it was my only choice if I wanted to skate again. I also continued to run, play tennis, etc. I started out by skating once a week for fun. I eventually competed in weekend time trials about once a month and an occasional masters' competition.

Although I was nervous at first about racing, I tried it anyway. It took me a couple of years to get a time below 45 seconds in the 500-meter race. According to the rules, once I skated a time below 45 seconds, I could compete in the longer races. Since I was competing a little more regularly, my times were improving nicely. By the end of the 2004–2005 racing season, I felt the need to compete more. I continued to race and train more intensely. I also continued to run 5K races, 10K races, half marathons, and an occasional triathlon. All of this led me back to competing and racing seriously again.

One of the issues I dealt with during this process of discovery was the fear, "What if they find out what I am really like?" This stems from my low self-esteem and my compensation for it. Although I have great self-esteem in some parts of my life, such as flying airplanes, I have poor self-esteem in others. For example, I worry about what people would think about me if they knew what I was really like, if they really knew what was going on in my head. Driven to accomplish a task, I get obsessive to the point of blocking out all else. This can be a great attribute at times like when I'm flying an airplane. However, by carrying that focus to extremes, I can let it cloud my priorities and decision-making. Balance is the key for skating as well as my thinking.

After sharing my thinking with some trusted friends and therapists, I realized that I was not so unusual. Getting down to it, a great deal of my thinking was just like everyone else's. There are more similarities than differences between me and the rest of the world. Not feeling so alone in my struggles, learning to open up more, I was encouraged by a close friend to make a list of wants and needs. I created this list with the idea that if I could name it, claim it, and put it out to the universe, I would have a better chance of seeing my desires coming to fruition.

My list of needs and wants included the need to share my life with someone who shared my way of thinking. My first wedding ceremony was in the Catholic Church. I was raised as a Methodist, but my first wife was Catholic, so we married in her church. Part of the ceremony was the lighting of a unity candle. The priest had a lit candle. He passed the flame on to both of us as we lit two separate candles. We used those tapers to light the unity candle together. This symbolized the union of our two flames. We then blew out our individual candles. That memory became a powerful symbol for me of one thing that had gone wrong in my life. By pouring all I had into the marriage for the sake of the marriage, I blew out my own identity. Now realizing I had lost it, I decided it was time to reclaim it.

We have a great deal of power in ourselves that we do not realize. Everything starts with a thought, which is followed by action, which usually reinforces the thought, and so forth. I have control over my thoughts and actions. They support each other. As a physical manifestation of what I think, I change my body by my thoughts. By deciding to eat healthy and work out, I change my body. I cannot change my DNA, but I can change how my body responds to my own actions and thoughts. I can choose an upward spiral or a downward one. Choosing is my accountability and responsibility.

The journey I have been on has provided me with a wealth of self-knowledge. Finally conscious to the world around me and to my part in it, I have developed a number of tools to deal with my life today and in the future. I am continuing to develop and refine the tools in my toolbox so that I can handle whatever comes my way.

CHAPTER WISDOM

Keep moving and be mindful, and you will put yourself into positions that will be right for you.

CHAPTER 2

AM I GOOD ENOUGH?

After a few years of slow but steady progress, I felt the need for more contact with this world on the ice and decided I was ready for the next step.

In May of 2004, I went to Calgary to order new skate boots. Dave Cruikshank, a three-time Olympian who was coaching at the Pettit Center in Milwaukee, recommended a friend of his, Scott Van Horne, for the job. I had been skating on old-technology skates and was willing to spend some money on new custom-fit, carbon-fiber boots and clap-mechanism skate blades. I anticipated that the new, stiff custom boots would help me go faster. I was ready to take a leap forward and commit to going faster. I flew to Calgary, where Scott took molds of my feet and started making my boots. Dave ordered some Viking blades from the Netherlands to complete the setup.

In a couple of months, I had the new equipment. I trained and raced the entire next season on these new skates. I took a little time to get used to the feel of the stiffer boots and no socks. It took all of about a minute to get used to the new clap mechanism. The previous generation of skates had blades that were fixed to the boots in two places, under the ball of the foot and at the heel. The new generation "clap" skates were bolted to a mechanism that had a hinge and spring in the front under the ball of the foot. Under the heel, there is a post attached to the blade only and not the boot. The push is started with the entire boot pressing down at both the ball of the foot and the heel. The finish of the push presses only on the ball of the foot, while the hinge and spring mechanism allows the boot to rise off the heel post. The distinctive sound of the skate, like hands clapping, is the skate blade returning to the heel after the blade comes off the ice, hence the name. The new technology facilitated a longer stroke, allowing the heel to rise while

PART ONE

the calf muscle continued the push to full extension of the leg. This new innovation fits the natural leg mechanics much better and allows a more natural application of power and recovery. All the top competitors use this skate technology.

By then, I was getting progressively faster each season. I had been racing in Milwaukee a few times during the 2004-2005 season and was doing pretty well. Calgary has one of the fastest rinks in the world, so I decide to try my new skates there at the end of the season in March 2005. During this competition, I went faster than I had ever gone on skates. My time for the 500-meter race was 40.99; the 1000-meter race was 1:22.47. As a comparison, at age 19, my fastest 500-meter race was 41.18 and my fastest 1000-meter race was 1:26.97.

In 2005, I was skating only once a week. How fast could I go if I put a full effort into training? After talking with Kirk Olson, a fellow skater, and his coach Dave Cruikshank, I entertained the idea of trying to qualify for the upcoming Olympic trails. I wanted to race with the elite skaters who were competing for spots on the upcoming Olympic team to go to Torino, Italy, for the 2006 Winter Olympic Games. I knew I could not make the team; I just wanted to be part of the elite group as I had been at age 19. At 48 years old, was it possible? I had to find out.

Inspired by this challenge, I asked to join Kirk as a training partner. Immediately, this quest made me feel very alive. Reconnecting with goals, progress, and achievement was something that drew me into the work. All of this also had a deeper meaning. I found not knowing where the journey was taking me scary and exhilarating at the same time. Something was leading me, and I knew that I must pay attention to this drive.

Kirk was 38 at the time, a husband and a father of three young boys. He was working a full-time job and training to attempt to make the Olympic team. He drove down from Appleton, Wisconsin, about the same distance as I drove up to Milwaukee from Kildeer, Illinois, to the indoor 400-meter oval to train on the ice. Kirk and Dave accepted me into their group, and I started training right away after I returned from Calgary in March 2005. I wanted to skate in the Olympic trials the following December. To be able to participate, I had to skate a qualifying time in a normal weekend race. I had about eight months to produce the necessary speed.

So a goal was clearly before me: skate a 39.0 second 500-meter race or better—or skate 1 minute, 18 second 1000-meter race or better. By accomplishing either one, I could skate both distances at the Olympic trials. The intention was to cut 2 seconds off my 500-meter time (which at that speed is about 30 meters) or 4.5 seconds off my 1000-meter time (or about 60 meters). I had never gone that speed, not even when I was 19 years old on the national team. To make my task even more daunting, the skaters and the qualifying times have gotten faster over the last few decades.

My brother, Olympic gymnast Bart Conner, gave me a book a couple of years ago written by Walter Anderson titled *Courage is a three letter word, and the word is YES*. I have heard that the Chinese symbol for courage is made up of two parts; one is danger, the other is opportunity. Some danger but more opportunity. I said, "YES!" I made the commitment to myself and announced it to the world.

I was training for my goal with a much different attitude this time than when I was 19, and it gave me a new zest for my sport. One of the biggest differences was having a full-time coach—Dave Cruikshank, a three-time Olympian and the husband of Bonnie Blair. Bonnie is the greatest woman speed skating sprinter of all time with five Olympic gold medals. Because I trusted Dave's judgment and knew that he could see me better that I could see myself, we moved forward. As I looked back after 30 years, I realized that, as a teenager, I had overtrained myself into the ground. This time, I was open to doing things differently. That attitude was very important. In order for me to change, I had to be willing to alter the way I think. Once I was open to change, amazing things were possible.

Taking the leap of faith that Dave knew skating and training better than I did was hard but necessary for my progress. In my youth, I worked for a season or two with long-distance coaches from Norway and the Netherlands (countries that excel in speed skating). Considering myself pretty smart about training, I thought I knew what was necessary for my development as a skater. As I look back, however, I realize I needed help with training, skates, and skating technique. Not having anybody to bounce ideas off of or to give me feedback so I could adjust when things started to go wrong was hard. As a youngster, I ran myself into the ground without knowing it.

The first couple of months training with Dave were spent on a stationary bike, between an hour and two a day. At first, just getting my body used to a lot of training volume was necessary. Even though I had been running and cycling for the last few years, now I was building up slowly to a much higher training volume and intensity. Then came Dave's training program in May: one day off per week, one and sometimes two workouts per day. Weight training every part of my body as well as my core would be necessary to go fast. My biggest fear was this: Could I recover enough between workouts to do the necessary volume of training? Being in shape is one thing. Skating shape is another level entirely. Transferring what I have built in strength and endurance to the ice is the true test.

My sport is speed skating, so I needed to learn how to skate faster than ever. This meant unlearning some of my old skating concepts and habits and dealing with some fears. Skating a turn at 35 miles per hour can be very scary while the skater is balancing on a thin, razor-sharp blade. Falling is a real possibility and a real danger. When skating really fast, we are on the edge of control. To push harder and go faster, we cross our own comfort zone into an area of new territory where the familiar becomes foreign. It is this boundary that must be pushed to consistently go faster.

Speed skating is a power sport. As I get stronger, I go faster and push the boundary towards more speed. The consequences of a fall can be either a minor embarrassment, possible injury to me or other skaters, or even a threat to my life. Learning to use proper technique when fatigued is essential to survival. While growing up, I thought I knew how to skate pretty well. Even so, training with Dave was taking my skating to a whole new level. But taking it to this next level meant making some very basic changes in the technical way to skate.

Speed skaters are great at cross training since that is most of our work, adapting as best we can because ice is not available year-round. Because of my high seniority at United Airlines as a Boeing 747 captain, I can be "on call" a great deal. If United calls me for an assignment, I go to work. If not, I have time to train for skating. I can do my off-ice training such as weight lifting, running, stationary bike almost anywhere, so I can train on a layovers as well as at home.

Both of my passions require me to fit all the pieces of the puzzle together to achieve the result I want. Both are as much about the process as the result. I find that rewarding. Because I am a big-picture kind of guy, seeing things from high up and then focusing on the specifics works well for me. That is why I am good at both of the pursuits I love.

The first priority for training was to build up my capacity for a heavy work volume. This was the early part starting in March through May. Then we added weight training and simulated-skating exercises. In late August, we were able to start skating in Milwaukee. The off-ice work was starting to translate to the ice. Feeling better than ever, I started doing some time trials to validate my work and to see where we could improve and change my technique. I was steadily improving but was still not good enough yet. In November, I went to Calgary—which has faster ice than Milwaukee—to get my qualifying time. I just missed it. Then a couple of weeks later, I flew to Salt Lake City to race in the weekly Saturday morning time trials.

Walking into the 400-meter indoor oval in Salt Lake City, Utah, is always an inspiring experience for a skater. It calls up memories of the Winter Olympic Games held there in 2002—the pomp, the pageantry, and the great stories of the athletes. The roof is suspended from beams and cables on the outside, creating a structure similar to a suspension bridge. Having the support outside the building leaves an uninterrupted open space inside that houses one of only twenty-nine indoor, oval, 400-meter tracks in the world. Inside the oval are two hockey rinks. Outside the oval is a running track as well as spectator stands and workout equipment. The building has many windows and great natural light. The temperature is about 60 degrees and there is no wind. The contrast between that environment and the one where I practiced

PART ONE

while I was growing up is staggering.

The Olympic oval at the Wisconsin State Fairgrounds in West Allis (a suburb of Milwaukee) was outdoors from the time it was built in 1968 until 1993. Wind, cold, and snow were a part of the landscape. One time it was so windy and cold that officials would not even let us out of the building to warm up for racing. That day, the wind chill was -50 F.

Sometimes it was so windy the snow fell sideways. I would be going so fast down the straightaway on the track with the wind behind me that it was hard to enter the turn and hold it very well. Then halfway through the corner, I would start skating into the wind, and it almost stopped me dead in my tracks. Wearing a knit muffler around my neck and covering my mouth might make air a little warmer so that inhaling would not burn my lungs. When I was able to grow a beard, it helped protect my face, but the ice clung to my mustache and beard from the exhalation of warm breath. At times, I simply could not wear enough layers. Deciding how to dress always involved a tradeoff. More layers would combat the cold, but they would sacrifice aerodynamic drag. Most of the difficulty in going fast comes from wind resistance. I decided speed was my prime consideration, so my nose, fingers, and toes were always cold.

Walking 50 yards from the outdoor ice surface back to the warm building, tired from the intense workout, was always a struggle. Cold in the extremities, especially the toes, made the walk difficult. After we got back in the building and found a place to sit down, taking off the skates was an exercise in pain management. Imagine unlacing the skates with frozen, numb fingers. Trying to speak with a numb face was frustrating, so it was best not to try until the muscles started warming up and working again.

Then we would peel off the skates to reveal toes that would not register any feeling for a while. We hobbled on our feet like so many penguins to get to the bathroom. Our toes did not work yet. Maybe a warm drink would help to warm hands, toes, and the insides. I trained nine months of the year off the ice by running, lifting weights, climbing hills, slide boarding, biking, etc. Then I would train intensely outdoors on a 400-meter long track for two months, always subject to the current weather conditions.

Perfect conditions never seemed to exist, certainly not during the time we were racing. If you made the team, you went to Europe and skated another ten weeks. That was most of my life in speed skating, working towards the goal of making the team to go to Europe.

To push, to glide, and to push again, this is what I love. Skating is not a natural movement; it is a learned activity. Learning the craft takes a very long time and is dependent on both time spent and natural talent. Skaters are always learning, changing, and growing. For me, nothing else compares to skating—the purity of it, the instant feedback. If I am not in skating shape, my body tells me right away. Skating hard intense laps becomes a struggle because of heaviness in my legs, which makes it difficult to maintain the low skating position that is needed to generate any real speed. If my head is not in the right place mentally to focus totally on skating, then my technique suffers and I go more slowly. If my emotions are clouding my vision, then my focus is not good and my technique and speed suffer. If I am not calm in my spiritual life, then I get ahead of myself with my expectations and my technique suffers—again sacrificing speed and endurance. I do this work because it is hard. I have always been driven this way.

The sport of speed skating has a purity, a black and white reality, pushing and gliding. The pushing is done by tilting the edge of the blade at an angle with the ice, toward the skater. This allows skaters to grip the ice and propel themselves forward. That move is a sharp contrast to the ease of gliding on the bottom. The sensation of gliding is like floating, suspended in time and space. Body position is essential for the efficient mechanics that create speed. Intense focus is necessary when a skater is going 35 miles per hour.

From the view of a spectator, the arm swing of a speed skater can be confusing. The basic purpose of the arm swing is for balance. As a person walks, he or she moves the arms as a counterbalance to the legs. In speed skating, at the beginning of a race during acceleration and hard pushing, both arms are used for balance. As the race continues, the need for counterbalance decreases. Typically during the turns, a skater will swing one arm and thus conserve energy as well as remain more aerodynamic. Skaters must always make a trade-off between energy expenditure and conservation. Every skater has a unique style of arm swing, and the differences can look dramatic.

As an example of my arm swing, in the 500-meter race, I swing both arms for the start and all straights. I choose to swing only my right arm in the turns for balance. I feel that my left arm interferes in the turn, so I leave it behind my back. In the 1000-meter race, I swing two arms during the start to the first turn, which is the first 50 meters. Then I swing one arm throughout the rest of the race until the last 50-meter straight, where I swing two arms for balance since I am very tired. In the 1500, I treat it the same way as the 1000 except that I swing two arms for the last 100 meters. In the 3000 or 5000, I will use two arms for the start, then one arm during the turns only, and no arms for the straights. Finally, two arms for the finish.

Playing crack the whip as a youngster creates much the same sensation as skating high speed turns. With a string of children hand in hand, one at the center and the rest strung out like the spoke of a wheel, the group spins and the last in line builds speed exponentially. We let go of the line at max speed, seemingly faster than our legs can carry us. Shot out of a cannon is the best way to describe it.

Before entering a turn in skating, I plan and spot the setup 30 meters before. Then I make the commitment, lean, and put pressure into the ice. In speed skating, we turn only left, counterclockwise around the ice track. When turning, we cross the right leg over the left and lean into the center of the track, counterbalancing the centripetal force. The faster we go, the more dramatic the lean. We create pressure into the ice as we lean, the right leg crossing over the left, which goes under our body towards the outside of the turn. We build crossover strokes to the middle of the turn where the apex is; the maximum centrifugal force is trying to push me to the outside of the track—or worse a fall. At max speed, I am always on the edge of control and abandon. A slight hesitation in the crossover strokes during the middle of the turn allows me to feel the forces of nature I am in concert with. Using my speed and leaning angle, I add my strength to accelerate out of the turn. Here is where weight training pays off. Perfect body position is essential at this speed. Coming out of the turn, I feel the crack-the-whip speed.

For the next 100 meters, I feel like I have been shot out of the cannon—and I cover the distance in 7 seconds. Without protective glasses, my eyes would not see through the wind-created tears. Eight straight-away strokes and then the next turn. Managing energy to get the most speed for the longest time and distance is the payoff. The wind in my ears, smell of the ice, speed, pressure, on the edge, consequences and results, internal and external, this is what skating is to me.

After I didn't make the team in December 1975, I amputated that part of my life. So here I was, walking into the Salt Lake rink on December 3, 2005. I had been slowly improving since my return to the sport and then training really hard since March when I committed to work toward these trials. But I was still not fast enough.

The rink in Salt Lake usually has the fastest conditions on the planet. This was one of my last real chances to qualify to skate in the Olympic trials and race with the elite skaters in the United States. To make the trials would be my "Olympics." My training partner Kirk Olson and I shared a hotel room, a rental car, and some great memories. The 500-meter race would be first that Saturday morning. There are two lanes on the track: the inner and the outer. Each skater has his own 13-foot wide lane, and he races against one other skater and the clock. In the 500, I started on the outer lane, skated the first outer turn, crossed over on the backstretch, and skated the second inner turn. The other skater in my pairing (usually referred to as my pair) did just the opposite. Building speed in the first outer turn can be tough because it has a larger radius than the first inner turn. The second inner turn has a smaller radius and at top speed can be very scary.

Approaching the starting line, I always repeat a mantra that helps me with my expectations. First, grateful to be here and skate. Then, confident that I have done the work. I will make adjustments as I go. I trust that I will get the results that I am supposed to get. Let go of the

PART ONE

outcome and the expectations, and stay in the moment of each movement.

That day, I had a good start off the gun and a pretty solid race, but I found it hard to hold the last inner turn. Still, I skated my all-time best time of 39.18 seconds! Four feet shy of qualifying. A good effort but not fast enough.

I had one more chance, the 1000-meter race, which is my best race. It fits my personality. I love to go fast. The top speeds on ice are generated in the 1000-meter race. I do not have the explosive speed for the 500, but I can get top speed and keep it longer than the pure sprinters can. I had about one hour between races to cool down, regroup and warm up again, getting as centered as possible to make it—or break myself trying. In this race, I was paired with Kirk, my training partner. He was skating the race just for training. He had already qualified for the trials and was working on endurance since he was a pure sprinter.

My old friend Nancy Swider-Peltz, Sr. would be calling my lap times to me and holding up a sign for additional visual reference for me. Nancy and I met when we were 12 years old and our families were two of the first twelve families that started the Park Ridge Speed Skating club in 1968. Nancy made eight Olympic trials in a row, competed on four Olympic teams, and has held numerous world records—accomplishing all that while having three children. She was now coaching her two kids and some others. She was there to help with my lap times and cheer me on. She knew intimately what was at stake.

I had the first inner lane, my favorite in this race. That meant I would also finish the last turn on the inner lane. We both started well, and since Kirk is a great sprinter, he went out hard. After the first 200 meters, we crossed the finish line with two laps to go. Kirk was ahead of me by about 20 yards. After the next turn, he lengthened his lead to about 40 yards. I kept my pace, knowing that he would start to fade at about the 600-meter mark. I built speed on the two next turns and started to close the gap. Coming down the last backstretch, I crossed over to the last inner turn. I had Kirk in my sights and would pass him going into the last turn. He heard me coming just from my breathing.

As I passed him, he said through his own gasps for oxygen, "Go, Bruce, go!" He knew I had a good race going. During that last turn, my vision started to get narrow, things were starting to go gray. That told me I was in oxygen debt, big time. Legs rubbery, straining to keep my balance. I was no longer consciously making skating turn strokes. I was only applying pressure to the ice as best I knew how. Not really conscious of skating, applying whatever strength I had to holding the turn and staying on my feet another 50 yards to the finish line. Coming out of the turn, needing to keep whatever speed I had for the remaining four strokes to the finish line. I stayed on my feet, straining for the line with all the extension I had.

Was it good enough? I forced myself to rise up to the vertical so I could glide, recover, and see the results. Through blurred vision, I saw a time of 1:17.47 on the scoreboard. I made it! I beat the qualifying time by 0.53 seconds! Translated into distance it was about 20 feet.

I could barely straighten up, barely breathe from the maximum effort. But I was floating. I had done it! I glided around for a couple of laps on the warm-up lane. A few skaters who knew what had happened, including Kirk and Nancy, gave me high fives. I gradually cooled down and got off the ice for an off-ice jog and stretch. I called my coach Dave back in Milwaukee to tell him what had happened and to share my success. I called my wife, my kids, my brothers, my father, and some very close friends. I spent a quiet moment speaking to my mother, who had passed away five years before. She was my biggest supporter when she was alive. I sensed her with me every step of that day. I felt her presence and strength. After my cool down and stretch, I went into the bathroom to change out of my skin suit, and something extra special happened.

I had experienced a certain exuberance when I made the decision to try for the trials. I just felt really alive when striving for a goal like this. Here, 30 years later, I was skating faster than ever. For years, I had questioned myself and what I was capable of doing. I was pretty good at my sport, but was I a champion? By age 14, I had accepted that my younger brother Bart was more successful than I was. I have no regrets about doing what I did to age 19, but I have always wondered how

PART ONE

good I could have been if I hadn't amputated that part of my life.

Alone in the spacious bathroom, I was able to really see myself in the bathroom mirror for the first time in my life and to look myself in the eye. I declared to myself aloud: "I am good enough!" At last, I accepted myself as I am. My father wrote a poem about me when I was about 16. I think he saw me for who I really was, even then. I am still that person today, although much more developed. One of my favorite parts is the following passage about self-esteem, self-respect, and self-image.

> Why does he stretch so? Who is he racing?
>
> The other skaters are already laughing and drinking hot chocolate.
>
> Does he race Olympic ghosts, McDermott and Blatchford?
>
> Or is he chased by his own image? And what does he hope to win?
>
> A fleeting flush of triumph? A medal or trophy?
>
> A record someone will break tomorrow?
>
> Or does he try to catch the goal of self-respect?

I admit I am very competitive and driven. Why? I don't know. I am just wired that way. Why did I do this? Not because it was easy, but because it was hard. I needed to see how far I could push myself. I know now that this attitude is not typical.

Now I have the answer. "I am good enough!" That moment of looking at myself in the mirror was pivotal for me. I knew then that I could set lofty goals, achieve them, and accomplish amazing things. That insight might seem odd to most people, considering what I have achieved so far in my life. However, my frame of reference was a younger brother who is an Olympic champion and the most accomplished male gymnast in U.S. history.

Yet, I am reminded that perspective is always relative. My brother Bart loves to joke about the fact that he and his wife Nadia Comenici have eleven Olympic medals between them, and he has two of them. So when he looks over at the other side of his own bed, he sees someone who has achieved more.

That day in Salt Lake, I was finally able to look at myself clearly and, from just competing against myself, I could say that I can set a goal and achieve almost anything. Now I could apply my newly found self-esteem and principles to all aspects of my life.

The things I learned about myself on this journey have been priceless. John Wooden, the famous basketball coach, has said, "Sports do not build character. They reveal it." I love the concept of pushing myself to see what I am made of.

I believe that pushing my limits has forced me to be honest with myself and, as a result, has revealed my true character. Just as the ancient alchemists used raw materials and heat to try to produce gold, I have used raw material of my personality and body, and added the stress and work and heat of change to produce a better me. The result in my external performance is measurable. The result inside me is priceless.

I used to define myself by my performance. I used to define myself by my job. I let others define me as well. They would say, "There's Bruce, the pilot." Through some tough times these last few years, I have learned that those definitions were very narrow. I no longer define myself by those things. I am way more than those narrow definitions. I now look at what I can bring to others, not what I have or what I can get.

I have learned a great deal during the process of reviewing my life to this point. I am grateful to share my story with you. By doing this review, I have already gained new perspective and, with that, new personal growth. This was a process I had to continue to find fulfillment in other areas—to get a complete life, to say I am good enough.

I am convinced that you too can achieve whatever it is you want.

PART ONE

We all have the ability. The question is whether we are willing to go for it and do the work necessary.

CHAPTER WISDOM
Core self-esteem is built from within and is not based on performance. Rather, it is the result of how we feel about ourselves.

CHAPTER 3
A PILGRIMAGE AND HEALING OLD WOUNDS

As a teenager, I dreamed of training and racing at the famous oval in Inzell, Germany. The rink is settled in between hills of the German Alps at 2,250 feet above sea level, protected from the wind by tall, snow-covered pines. The 10,000-seat stadium provides the backdrop for the best racing in the world. Many world records have been set and broken at this iconic landmark of speed skating. I learned in 2009 that the local authorities would be shutting the rink down in a couple of months to rebuild the rink into an indoor "ice-hall." This would be the last opportunity to skate outdoor at Inzell. The organizing body for International Masters Speed Skating had scheduled the first-ever World Masters Sprint Championships for February 14-15, 2009.

I had been competing regularly since qualifying for the Olympic trials in 2005. In addition, I had set a few world records for masters in my age group. I found myself stepping off the airplane in Munich to compete in Inzell as a master. When I made the commitment to this trip, I did not know the full impact it would have on my life. I needed to know from the bottom of my soul, without a shadow of a doubt, whether I was good enough to produce at the exact time when it mattered most. Just like those Olympians who can produce their best performance during the Games. Many other people in my life had told me I was good enough, but I needed to prove it to myself. This was one of those deep down questions I had been asking myself since a very early age.

Short track speed skating is where all the skaters start on the starting line together and do several laps until they reach the length of the race, from 500 to 1500 meters. Typically the ice is a hockey rink with an oval track set up so that one lap equals 111 meters. Whoever crosses the finish line first wins. It is very exciting to watch because it requires a great deal of strategy, timing, and tactics. You can be a great skater but lose because of poor tactics. You can be the strongest skater and still be taken out by someone else making a bad pass. You can be in the right time and the right place to win, even if you are not the strongest or best. Chance often influences what happens.

Short track can also be very dangerous. A skater going 30 miles per hour must try to avoid colliding with razor-sharp blades, flying elbows, and padding on the edge of the ice. Required safety equipment is helmets, neck guards, and Kevlar-reinforced socks.

In contrast, long track is done on a 400-meter track with two racing lanes. Only two skaters race at a time, each in a separate lane. Each lane is about 4 meters or 13 feet wide. Each skater goes all out for the best time he or she can get. When everyone is finished racing, the best time wins. I like having my own lane. I am a purist: me, the clock, and one other skater. Having my own space to be able to get my maximum push into the ice without interference is important to me. I feel my own soul when I am racing this way; it is an inward journey for me. I have been drawn to it since age 16. That is when I decided not to compete in short track racing anymore. Long track can still be dangerous—the speeds are higher, more like 35+ miles per hour—but for me, it is more of a controlled risk. At least, not so much chaos.

In December 1975, when I was 19, I trained at the outdoor 400-meter long track in Milwaukee. I missed the U.S. team that year by two spots, so I was not able to travel to Inzell, Germany, or other European rinks with the team. At that point, I retired from the sport, wondering whether I was really good enough. Burned out and overtrained, I continued my college studies, took flight instruction, married, began my flying career, and started a family.

After I retired from skating at age 19, my legs ached every day for 18 months. Wow, was I overtrained! I had worked so hard as a teenager without being very smart about what I was doing because I had no one to tell me to slow down and rest. So I trained harder than anyone else, ran myself into the ground, and didn't even know it. No one could have told me how to stop, slow down, or even taper off back then anyway because I thought I knew what was best for me.

For five years after I retired, I did nothing physical like jogging or cycling. In retrospect, I see that I needed that time to heal physically, mentally, emotionally, and spiritually. Then I got an itch. I felt like moving again and started jogging, slowly at first. As a commuter pilot in Arkansas, I discovered jogging around was healing somehow. Leery about my overtraining tendencies, I remained very tentative. After a couple of years, a friend said he was going to do a triathlon and wondered if I might like to try it. "That might be cool," I answered. I was a pretty good runner and a better biker, so if I worked on my swimming, I might be ok. I had a goal again, which was important. It probably fed me more than I realized at the time. I had achieved a great deal in my flying career by then, and I needed something more.

I had tasted a new way of feeding my need for sport, for goals, for achievement, for activity. Over the next few years, I competed in 5k races, 10k races, half marathons, and several triathlons. I was running on almost every flying layover, also running at home occasionally to keep my two Labrador retrievers in shape.

As a pilot, to keep flying I have to take a physical exam every six months with a Federal Aviation Authority (FAA) medical examiner. If I do not pass this medical exam, I lose my ability to be a pilot and thus my career. Staying in shape is part of my job.

Approaching 40, I was in the middle of the pack of racers. Competing against guys who were not married or had kids was tough. Those guys trained a lot. It became important for me to get back into something I was good at—and that meant skating. I began to want to tread water again in the pool that I had fled so quickly when I was 19.

After all the years away, I was ready to see what skating was like. Surely, I was much older and wiser now. After enough time away, I could approach skating in a different way. I had vastly different expectations now; hell, I was over 40. Drawn back to skating, was I somehow trying to resolve unfinished business? Anyone who knew me and my

PART ONE

history could probably see my issues a mile away. Because I was too close, I could only faintly recognize them. Creeping very slowly at first, as my skating improved, I set higher goals. After the 2005 Olympic trials, I wanted and needed to achieve more because I still had a lot in my tank.

So I traveled to Germany. This would be the first-ever World Championships for masters in the sprint races. We would race 500 meters and 1000 meters each day, Saturday and Sunday, and the total of all four races would determine the world champion. Already holding the world record in my age group for the 500 meters set at Calgary the previous season, I was an obvious favorite. Still, I had to show up and produce.

Maripat (my girlfriend at the time, now my second wife) and I flew from Chicago to Munich nonstop, leaving on Monday night, arriving Tuesday morning. Maripat and I had been living together for a couple of years by then, so it was essential that she come along for support. We rented a car and drove about 90 minutes to the sleepy little town of Inzell where the rink was.

Many world records have been set and broken at this picturesque setting. The elevation is about 2,250 feet above sea level, so Inzell is not considered either a high-altitude rink or a sea-level rink. Higher-altitude rinks are faster due to less air resistance. The outdoor setting among the foothills of the German Alps was spectacular. The hills are very steep and close to the stadium. This provided a great windbreak. When there is hardly any wind to interfere with skating, times can be very fast. The great pine trees that surrounded the stadium and the snow-covered terrain added atmosphere to the setting.

We rented a room at the bed and breakfast where my coach Dave Cruikshank had met his wife Bonnie Blair. After we met Heidi and Albert Eckart, our hosts, we settled down for a nap. After we woke up, we decided to drive around the town, get some food for the kitchenette, and see the rink. The rink was about a 15-minute walk away, but we decided to drive so that I could conserve my energy for skating and racing.

We took the main road through town to the rink where the exit sloped down to the parking lot. Nestled down in the valley was the famous Inzell rink. We entered the stadium and walked down some stairs to the ice. It was snowing lightly with a light wind, creating a winter wonderland. The snow was a nice powder that covered everything. On the ice, it was only about an inch deep, and I could barely see the ice surface underneath. Looking at the stands, I saw that the snow cover was a couple of feet thick. The structure around the rink had many functions. Part of the structure housed the ice machines and the plows to keep the ice clear of snow and to resurface. Grandstands occupied most of the perimeter around the rink. The icehouse that housed the officials, timers, and scorekeepers was built into the stadium stands. Some of the stands were covered to protect spectators from the elements. I could jog in the area behind the stands where the stadium roof kept the snow away.

A hockey rink was located on the inside of the oval, and a tunnel led under the oval to get there. The skaters had nice, heated locker rooms under the stands to put on skates and warm up. Just outside of the grandstand were a bar, a restaurant, and a coffee shop. Maripat and I decided to go there to get an espresso and warm up. The restaurant's interior walls displayed memorabilia from competitions and skaters of the past. This was a place steeped in history, stories, and traditions, and it left me in awe and very reverent.

We went back to our apartment and then decided to walk around town to find some dinner. The town had a number of great authentic German restaurants to choose from as well as Greek, Italian, and Chinese. We found a German restaurant and sat down. The menu was in German with an English translation. Our waitress spoke English like most, but not all, locals. We learned that she was from Alaska and had married a German and had settled in Inzell a number of years before. She was very helpful, and it was nice to make a local connection of sorts. During the week, we sampled many of the local restaurants.

The next day after breakfast, I went to the rink to skate. A little excited, but a little wary. I remembered all too well the bone-chilling cold of practice sessions in years past. I had purchased some warmer clothing for this event. Neoprene skate covers that fitted over my skate boots were essential equipment for the cold. My custom molded carbon-fiber skate boots do not allow for socks. Skating indoors is never an issue with these skates, but without some protection at Inzell, my feet would really freeze. I need to feel my feet to sense the ice and the pressure I'm applying to it. In addition, I wore a lot more clothing than normal, my regular skating tights but added an extra layer of lined warm-up pants. On top, I had on several more layers than normal and heavier gloves and hat than I was used to.

My skating protective glasses were essential to keep the snow out of my eyes. Just like ski goggles, they have yellow lenses that help skaters see the ice and snow. A couple of inches of fluffy powder covered the ice. I was used to seeing the ice surface, but it was not possible that day or the rest of the week. The overcast and continuous snow (it snowed about 2 1/2 feet that week) provided a less-than-cheery yet cozy atmosphere. Adjusting to the cold and snow, I modified my training to come into the locker room to warm up periodically.

Familiar masters skaters from all over the world were showing up now. Maripat was there to cheer me on and accompany me when I came in to warm up. Three other American skaters were there: John Diemont from California, in the 60 - 64 age group; Mark Chrysler from Salt Lake City, in the 50-54 age group with me; and finally, Brian Boudreau from Boston but living and working in Salt Lake City, in the 40-44 age group. We laughed about traveling half way around the world to feed our passion for skating and racing. The plan was to train and prepare for the upcoming weekend of racing. Meeting for dinner several times that week helped us make strong bonds through this mutual experience.

Making adjustments for the snow and the inability to see the ice very well through the thin powder was critical. My prep work involved timing each stroke for the slower outdoor ice and making mental notes about visual markers for turn entries. About two weeks prior to leaving for this meet, I had pulled a groin muscle. Doing a start without aggravating my injury would be tricky. I tried to do a minimum number of practice starts to save the muscle, but enough to get the timing right. I learned not to explode off the starting line but to skate smoothly. This forced me to push more down into the ice earlier in the start. I had to warm up very slowly and to be very careful about any overextension.

The week prior to any major competition is tough for me. The week in Inzell was especially challenging. When I was growing up, if a skater made the team, he or she could travel to Europe and the world-famous German rink to train and race with the best skaters in the world. Gliding around the rink in Wisconsin, talking to those who had made the trip to this wonderful place, I sensed a certain mystique about Inzell. The mountains, the pines, the great ice, the big stadium. Quite a contrast to the wind-swept Wisconsin rink by the expressway and cement plant, where the parents of skaters stood by the ice to watch, then went inside quickly to warm up. Since I had never made the team, this trip was like a pilgrimage for me. It was what I had dreamed of as a young skater.

Yet, because of my injury, it was important for me to do easy work that week. The time in Inzell was also supposed to be fun and the trip of a lifetime. I have a tough time balancing competing needs like that, especially when my ego gets involved.

So the preparations went forward for the week. Skating Wednesday, Thursday, Friday in the snow. On Friday afternoon, we drove to a nearby town. We got lost in a snowstorm. Returning to Inzell should have been a quick trip of about an hour but took about 2-½ hours instead. As a result, we had quite an adventure in the German countryside.

Friday evening, we went to the opening draw at the town hall. The draw lasted about an hour, and at the conclusion, the organizers offered appetizers and drinks for a social hour. I was able to see whom I would be racing with for the first day's 500- and 1000-meter races and what lanes I would be starting in.

We met our American friends for some relaxing conversation before the big event. The guys had just been to Norway and Holland, skating and watching World Cup events, cheering on the U.S. team. The speed skating community is pretty small in the United States, and almost everyone at this level, even the masters, knows everyone else. I remember skating with John Diemont when I was a teenager. I was also able to make some new skating friends and reconnect with some who had been in Calgary at the World Masters All-Around Championships the year before. I had a pretty good reputation around the masters world because I had made the Olympic trials in 2005.

Saturday came and breakfast before racing. Warm up off the ice by jogging around the rink in the snow. I stretched under the stadium roof back behind the stands in a nice flat spot where there was no snow. The 500-meter race would come first. The sky was still overcast, just as it had been all week. Light snow fell, and about a 10-mph wind blew down the home straightaway. About 1/2 inch of powder covered the ice. This would slow things down, so I would probably not set any records.

The entire competition was done by racing in quads—groups of four, rather than pairs. The reason is that we had 165 skaters from 25 countries competing in 5-year age groups, starting at 30 and ending at 85+. The only way to finish in a reasonable time each day was to run two skaters first, then immediately start two more skaters. Four skaters approached the starting line at a time. The first two would go to the starting line while the next two waited about 5 meters back. As soon as the first pair began racing, the next pair was called to the line and started. By the time the second pair started, the first pair was about halfway around the track. If the second pair committed a false start, they stepped off to the warm-up track to let the first pair go by and finish their race. Then the second pair could be started. As long as there were not too many false starts, the meet could run very well and very fast. The same was done for the 1000-meter race. I don't know of any time that one skater overtook another in the previous pair. Of course, these were short sprint races. In longer distances, some overlap and passing occurs when quads are run. It is up to the officials to keep everyone straight, and they always do a great job.

Both days started around 9:30 and finished by 2:30. Paired with a Norwegian I had raced against in Calgary in 2007, I had the inner first turn in my first 500. After making a pretty good start, I never saw him after the first 50 meters. I never have to worry about being motivated for a race; when the gun goes off, I just go like hell, keeping my emotions and expectations in check, staying in the moment. At Inzell, I did the best I could and trusted that the results would be exactly as they were supposed to be. Maripat cheered for me from the edge of the ice halfway down the homestretch. She has a great, clear cheerleader's voice. I won the first 500 race in my age group by about 1/2 second. The time was not as fast as I was used to clocking indoors. This race was more about the time relative to my competitors.

After the first race, I did a proper cool-down skate, then an off-ice jog and stretch. We had about 3 hours before my next race, so we went back to the bed and breakfast for some rest and lunch. I relaxed for a while and replayed the race a few times in my head. We went back to the rink after lunch to repeat what I had done that morning for the 1000-meter race. The conditions were still the same.

Paired with another Norwegian, I was starting in the outer lane. The pairings and positions for the first day's racing had been drawn the night before. I made a pretty good start again, trying to be careful not to re-pull my groin. After a couple of good laps, I was giving it my all, skating more from muscle memory than anything else since none of my normal visual cues were there. I won that race with my pair by a nice margin. I also won my age group by another nice distance. Totaling up my time so far, I found that I had a pretty commanding lead on the rest of the field. In fact, I was ahead of the next younger age group, 45-49.

After the normal routine of skating cool down, off-ice jog, and stretch, we went back to the bed and breakfast, then out to dinner with the fellow Americans. Then I sharpened my skates, which usually takes about 45 minutes. I usually sharpen them before each race day to make sure that my skates are as perfect as possible. Doing so takes one more variable out of the equation and gives me the best possible result. Confidence in my equipment is always essential.

During the two-day competition, all the skaters were required to start each race (both the 500 and the 1000) from each starting lane,

PART ONE

one on Saturday and the other on Sunday. The pairings for the last two races on Sunday would be based both on lane placement and the standings after the first day of racing. As a result, I would be paired with my closest competitors who needed the opposite lane. This would in effect pair me with the fastest racers and assure me of good competition in each of the last two races.

Saturday night I did not sleep well. I have a tendency to try and figure out every conceivable problem and options for solving them. I usually need some extra time to settle down after a day's racing. I was not worried about being too tired for Sunday. The fact of this being the first World Masters Sprint Championship would be enough to get my adrenaline going for the next day's racing.

Sunday's weather started out the same as all the other days that week with overcast skies and light snow. While I was doing my normal jog around the rink in the snow, I stopped by the official posting of the results from the previous day. As I saw that I was in first place by a nice margin, the Italian masters coach approached me. He asked if I was Bruce. I said yes, and he introduced himself. He said that he had heard of me qualifying for the Olympic trials in 2005, which was an inspiration to him and his fellow skaters. I was floored! I did not know that my story had been told outside the United States. He told me that he had seen me on TV and read articles about me. I thought it was pretty cool that my story had reached much farther than I had ever dreamed. I was not doing this for notoriety but for passion and the love of the sport. Even so, my step was a little lighter after that.

Paired with Victor Van den Hoff in the 500, I had the outer lane this time. The previous year, Victor had won the Masters All-Around in Calgary for our age group. I had won the 500 in Calgary and set a world record. He won the 1500, and I placed second (a very pleasant surprise to me). He then won the 3000 and the 5000 to win the overall. He was a national team member in Holland just as I was in my teens in the United States. Here we were a few decades later, still passionate about skating and racing.

I had a pretty good opening 100 meters on the outer lane, then after the turn, I beat Victor to the crossover. I was about 20 meters and 1 second or better faster than him. I knew I had him beat for the championship at that point and all I had to do was finish the job. Set up the last inner turn and hang on. With my focus on each stroke, I finished well ahead. I felt confident as I crossed the finish line but not ready to celebrate just yet, not with another race to skate. As my fellow Americans and Maripat's distinctive, clear voice cheered me on, I won the third of four races. I glided around the warm-up lane, put on my warm-ups, did a few more cool-down laps, and then got off the ice. While jogging around the rink, I slowly gained a full sense of what was happening to me.

Maripat and I watched our fellow Americans race. John and Brian had some good results, but Mark had pulled out after the first day because he didn't feel well. The sun started to peek out from behind the thinning overcast. I was talking to Victor while watching some races, and he said that usually one race at Inzell would be in great conditions. He was right. We returned to the rink a couple of hours later for the final 1000 meters, and iconic Inzell lived up to its reputation. The overcast broke up and the clouds vanished. The sun shone on perfect ice. The wind was but a whisper. The surrounding mountains and snow-covered pines looked like a winter-wonderland picture post card.

Victor and I were in second and first place in our group, so we were paired together for the final 1000-meter race. I would start and finish on the inner turn, my favorite. I did a normal warm up off and on the ice, still being careful about my groin pull. I could see Victor from my vantage point at the start. When we came around at the first 200-meter mark, I was about 10 meters in front. The next turn is pretty tricky at such high speed, but I took it well. We crossed over and skated the next turn almost side by side. Maripat told me after the race that he looked like he really wanted to win one race and knew this was his chance. We crossed the 600-meter mark with one lap to go, and I was still ahead but only by a couple of feet. We skated the next turn, and he passed me and beat me to the crossover. He was now about 20 meters in front of me going down the backstretch. But I had the advantage of the last inner turn being about 15 meters shorter than the outer. Victor

PART ONE

could not see me, but I had him in my sights. I love to chase a competitor down on the last turn. Because I had qualified for the 2005 trials like this, I knew I could do it again.

I set up my last turn and went for it. I passed him about two-thirds of the way through the turn, then we came out of the turn with 50 meters to go and I was about 15 feet ahead. I concentrated on my strokes. My legs were near exhaustion, heart racing, max breathing for survival. *Just stay on your feet, Bruce! You could win this!* Victor put up a last valiant charge and closed the gap to about 5 feet. We crossed the line, and I immediately looked to my right to see where he was. We acknowledged each other. We stood up and glided towards the inside warm-up track. I reached over to shake his hand for a race well done. He had given all he could that day, and so had I. I raised my arms in victory as I glided on the warm-up track. Maripat was beside herself with excitement. She contributed to my success as much as anyone in my network of support, and she deserves credit for her part.

I put my warm-ups back on and skated over to Maripat at the edge of the ice, where she gave me biggest hug and kiss I could ever remember. She was beaming and knew what had happened to me out on the ice better than I did. I was just waking up to it. Normal cool down on the ice, now these were victory laps. I wanted to stay out there forever, so I did a few extra laps soaking up the experience as much as possible. The sun was shining all over the world for me, especially in Inzell.

I did my normal off-ice jog but with an even lighter step, wondering if my feet were even touching the ground. I had put a log on the fire of my own self-esteem.

As I received my award the on the podium, I was standing on the shoulders of all my supporters. By qualifying to compete at the Olympic trials in Salt Lake in 2005, I realized I could skate faster than ever. Traveling to Inzell and living out the teenage dream of skating and beating the best created the deep down satisfaction of knowing I was great. I was now a masters world champion. With my talent and drive, I knew I could produce when it counted most.

Coming to grips with the significance of this trip, I realized I had experienced some very deep wounds as a teenager. By amputating the skating part of my life, I had blocked out and denied what had transpired in 1975. After pouring so much effort into that season and my career, it was disheartening to think that all of my effort had not yielded the results I wanted. Now, by going back 33 years later, I could now see what happened to me then, and since. With a much wider view, I now had the tools to look at the situation and the emotional strength to handle it. It came at the exactly the right time for me. I was able to bolster my self-esteem and self-image in the process, and heal the deep wound of my 19-year-old self, thus becoming whole again.

After this pivotal experience, I could now rest with the idea that I can produce when I need it most. I would continue to compete for the love of competition, not from the need to prove anything. This was a hard-fought victory that gives me peace and serenity that outlives the need to prove anything to anybody else, especially myself.

CHAPTER WISDOM

By taking small steps every day, we exercise courage to heal our old wounds from within and to become whole.

PART ONE

CHAPTER 4

THE LOVE OF A FATHER

Remember the few lines from my father's poem that I shared in Chapter 2? Here is the entire poem my father wrote about me when I was about 16 years old. He had hopes that I would be an Olympian then.

SPIRIT OF '76 -- OLYMPIC SPEED SKATER

Stark lean silhouette against a darkening sky
Measures effortlessly the ice in ten meter strides.
An imaginary track precisely surveyed in his mind
Guides his turn and glide strokes in mock slow motion.
Each movement carefully calculated to maximize the thrust
With arms reaching out, pulling back, swinging high behind.
Each foot under body center starts
Gigantic leg strokes too long for the horizontal torso.

Seventeen inch blades cut the ice subtly
So sharp they could easily shave the peach fuzz from his chin.
Breathing as measured as the pace stroke -And heart rhythmically beating to match.
Muscles flexible in spite of the cold,
Straining to balance the relentless press of spirit.

Why does he stretch so? Who is he racing?
The other skaters are already laughing and drinking hot chocolate
Does he race Olympic ghosts McDermott and Blatchford?
Or is he chased by his own image?
And what does he hope to win? A fleeting flush of triumph?

A medal or trophy? A record someone will break tomorrow?
Or does he try to catch the goal of self-respect

The lake ice is never smooth
With unforgiving cracks to keep his mind alert.
A chilling gust keeps balance honest.
Powdery shavings and grooves show other skaters have gone
   this way
Were all so highly motivated? Or so stubborn?
Did they feel the pleasant numbness-Not of cold but of tendons too stretched?

He counts six more full-effort laps.
Is this enough to beat the best?
Unsure, he fast-paces eight more.
A swirl of light snow blends with him at the far turn.
High flying geese seek a cornfield - not these icy shores.

Honk from a patient parent's car calls him.
He slows, straightens, and circles to let the real world return.

H. W. Conner

One of my favorite parts is the passage about self-esteem, self-respect, and self-image.

This has been part of my struggle throughout my life. I want to please my father, but the core issue is about my own self-respect. So I must earn my own respect, somehow. Sports, specifically speed skating, have provided the perfect method for me to do just that. Speed skating is a way for me to do something of value to me, to pursue my goals, and to boost my core self-esteem. Healing from the past was an added benefit of using speed skating as the method of my plan.

My flying career is another example of how I found my path and broke down barriers. When I got my first pair of glasses at the age of 16, an eye doctor told me that I would never fly airplanes for a living.

PART ONE

As a boy, I had decided to be a major airline pilot. Growing up not far from O'Hare airport in Chicago, seeing the airplanes flying in and out of O'Hare, I wanted to know what was going on in the cockpits of those airplanes. I used to get rides to Milwaukee to skate with a friend. His father was an American Airlines pilot. He was a guy who loved his job, made a good living, and was around his family a great deal. I could aspire to that kind of life.

Looking back at family movies, I see that I always had a model airplane in my hand. I loved building those models. Going back even further, I remember that my father had a job just after graduating from the University of Kansas as a structural engineer for North American Aviation. He was involved with analyzing structural components of aircraft fuselages. He worked on the X-15 project, the F-100, the F-86, and some rocket projects. My father drew my birth announcement of a futuristic fighter jet that looks a great deal like the present day F-22.

The designers and engineers listed on my birth announcement blueprint were Harold and Jackie Conner (my parents). The special con-

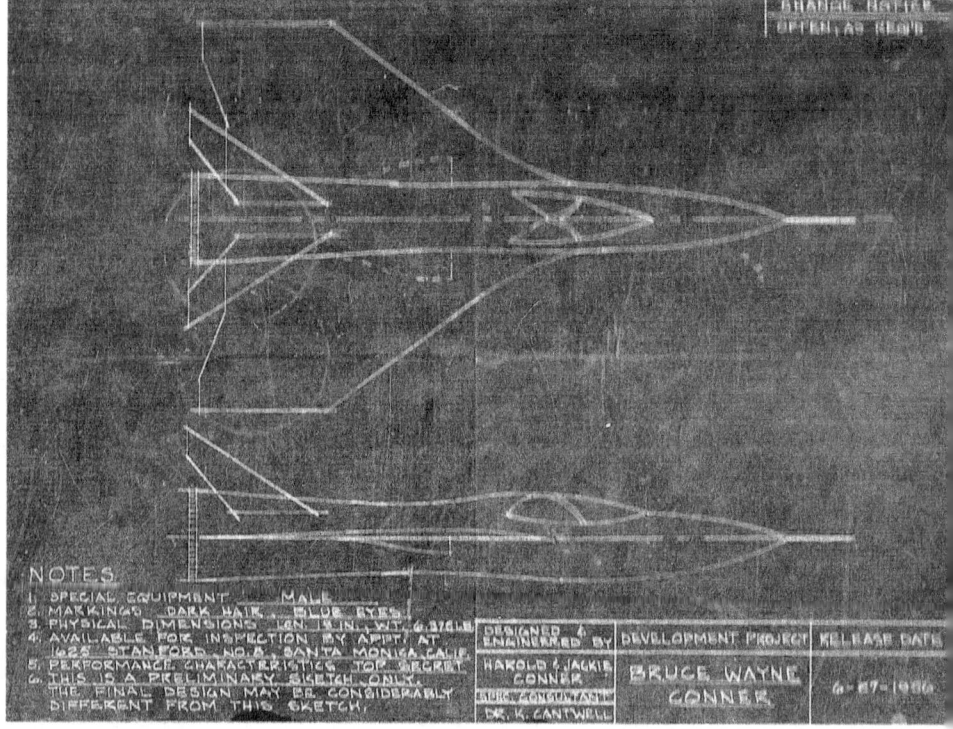

sultant was the doctor who delivered me. My specifications were my length and weight: 19 inches and 6.375 pounds. My release date was my birthdate: 6/27/1956. Special equipment was "MALE." Markings were "Dark hair, Blue eyes." Available for inspection at the trailer park in Santa Monica where my parents lived. Performance characteristics were "top secret." Also a note said, "This is a preliminary sketch only, the final design may be considerably different from this sketch." Wonder what it was that drew me to aviation?

In high school, I applied for a spot for the Air Force Academy in Colorado Springs. The recruiter told me that because I wore glasses, flying would not be an option for me. His remark made it obvious that the military was not the way to go.

My father and I found Gateway Tech. It is a small college in Kenosha, Wisconsin, where I could learn to fly and get an associate's degree. I learned to fly while still training for the 1976 Olympic trials. Gateway Tech was halfway to the rink in Milwaukee, a perfect location. I graduated with all my flying certificates and an associate's degree after two years. Correspondence courses allowed me to add a bachelor's degree later while flying as a commuter pilot.

My flying career started by teaching flying and moving my way up through flight instructing and the commuter airlines. One major carrier told me that since I did not have perfect vision, I did not meet their requirements. Why the strict requirement? The response was they could throw half of the job applications in the trash, which made their selection process easier. At that time there were many more pilots than jobs, and competition was fierce. I did not pick United; they picked me. In fact, I applied to all of the major carriers and none accepted me except United. By putting it out to the universe and persevering, I eventually reached my goal. I finally reached the top of my field as a Boeing 747-400 captain, flying all over the world.

As much as I love and respect my father, working to please him was only a start to the key of self-motivation and achievement. I had to dig down deep within myself to find the motivation to really excel in life. Sibling rivalry with my two younger brothers, especially Bart, was also a factor in my young development. The family dynamic set up an environment where all of us in the family, including my parents, valued achievement and the journey. The support network was constructed for us and fostered along the way, so each of us could benefit by goal setting, achievement, and learning through the journey.

The benefit of strong parents who supported our efforts was undeniable. As an adult, I have set myself up for the best situation in terms of achievement and growth.

If you had the proper motivation and support, what would you do with it? By creating your own environment you set the stage for future successful living. What do you want your future to look like? What dreams do you want to fulfill? My hope is that you use the remaining chapters of this book to move closer to achieving those goals. Break down your barriers while journeying toward wholeness.

CHAPTER WISDOM

We are not alone. We have the benefit of many resources, seen and unseen, to help us get past our barriers, internal and external.

CHAPTER 5

ASKING FOR WHAT I NEED FROM THE UNIVERSE

My personal life had been a rocky journey the last few years. In August 2005, I moved out of the house I lived in with my first wife. I could no longer live with my spouse due to irreconcilable differences. We continued marital therapy for a few more months. Realizing that we could not reconcile, we started mediation, and eventually I filed for divorce after a few months. We negotiated and finally finished the process three years later, ending a 31-year marriage. During this period, our son finished college; he now has a career of his own and lives in Chicago.

My daughter was having difficulty in high school because of the family turmoil. We agreed to change her environment, so she and my soon-to-be ex-spouse moved a few miles away to another high school district for a fresh start. My daughter did better in high school as a result of the move.

But how would the change affect me? I didn't really want to leave the house in Kildeer where we had lived for 15 years. It was in a heavily wooded area but still close to everything, and I loved it. We had put the house on the market after I filed for divorce, and I had moved back into the house until it sold. After refinishing the kitchen and office wood floors, I had the house in great shape. Unfortunately the housing market crashed, and after one year on the market, the house still had not sold. Since I had been paying the mortgage all along and continuing to live there while we negotiated our divorce, I retained the house in our settlement. Today, I still live in the house I love. I could not have made a better plan. After I put my desire to stay in my home out to the universe and kept moving my feet, I ended up keeping the house. The

PART ONE

circumstances of my divorce and the timing of the housing market crash created a result I could not have planned.

According to most of my friends who had gone through divorces before me, the new woman in the relationship does not feel comfortable in the marital house. That was not the case with Maripat. She loves the house and does not feel any of the leftover turmoil of my past marriage; she senses only my positive presence.

As for meeting Maripat, this is what happened. When I moved into an apartment in 2005 at the start of my divorce process, I knew that I needed to be alone for a while. I was slowly starting to feel better, but I had a lot of work to do on myself to be a better partner. When the dust started to settle in my life, I could see a clearer way and what the landscape looked like around me. Creating a list of traits to look for in a partner was one task I needed to do. Making a list of things to work on for myself was another. After about nine months by myself, I realized that I was a valuable person to be with and that I had a lot to offer. A relationship was no longer going to define me, but it would add to my life. It was important for me to be connected to a woman in an intimate way. A friend of mine fixed me up with someone. I was terrified since I had not dated since high school.

After one steady dating relationship for a few months failed to work out, I needed to be alone again to work out some issues. Part of my plan was defining what I was looking for in a long-term relationship and putting that out to the universe. I prayed, meditated, and stayed positive with faith that the universe would answer.

I was scheduled to fly a six-day trip to Hong Kong and Singapore on September 21, 2007. Running a bit late that morning due to road construction, I pulled into the employee parking lot to catch the company bus that took us across the airport to United flight operations. I saw the employee shuttle bus traveling through the lot and parked near the last stop. I don't normally park there but did not want to wait 15 minutes for another bus. As I approached the bus, I noticed a flight attendant running to catch it from farther away. I waved to the bus driver that someone else was coming. I got on the bus, put my bags in the racks, and sat down. The flight attendant put her bags in the racks as well. As the bus started to pull away from the stop, she lost her balance and inadvertently sat in my lap. "Hello," I said in surprise. She rose, sat next to me, and said, "Hello." Her name was Maripat.

She went on to say that she was a little nervous because she was on reserve and was assigned to fly to Hong Kong today on her birthday. I said "Happy Birthday, I will fly you to Hong Kong."

Maripat answered, "Thank you, but you look too young to be a 747 captain." She thought that I might be a captain on a 737 (a much smaller domestic jet).

After assuring her that I was the captain on the trip that day and would be flying her to Hong Kong, I said that I would see her in the flight attendant briefing. As we rode the bus to the terminal, we talked for a few more minutes and discovered that we lived about a 15-minute drive away from each other in the northwest suburbs of Chicago.

I showed up at the flight attendant briefing as usual to introduce myself and brief the chief purser and the flight attendants about the flight that day. As it turns out, Maripat was assigned to work the upper deck because of her low seniority of only three years with United. The upper-deck flight attendants take care of the twenty-six business-class passengers there, as well as the four pilots on the flight deck.

On that particular flight, my primary first officer on the six-day trip to Hong Kong and Singapore had brought along his wife. He had been in Iraq for the past few months, serving our country by flying airplanes for the military. Recently reunited, the couple wanted to spend some time together, so she joined us on the trip. Maripat found out where she was sitting and took her some extra snacks. During the flight, Maripat and I started get to know each other.

After we landed in Hong Kong, we all rode on the crew bus to our hotel on Victoria Island. It was about a 45-minute ride. Maripat and I sat near each other and started to talk more about our similarities. We discovered that we had both married people we met in high school and were both in the middle of divorcing. We both had been living separately from our soon-to-be ex-spouses for a few years.

On the bus going into downtown Hong Kong, we continued to

PART ONE

find more similarities. We had been going through a similar scenario of divorce, living separated, and dating. We both had chocolate Labrador retrievers; we both had two children; the list went on.

After we arrived at the hotel, my three first officers asked Maripat out for a birthday drink. Maripat, the other three pilots, my first officer's wife, and I met in the lobby about an hour after check in. We walked about ten minutes to a local hangout for United crews. It was an English pub that was very busy because the World Rugby Championship was being played in Hong Kong and broadcast on TV. After a short while, the rest of the crew decided they were going to go on to other places. I told Maripat that I was not interested in going out with the others but wanted to go next door to a good Mexican restaurant. Would she like to join me? She said yes, and we went to have dinner.

We continued to talk and get to know each other. I was definitely feeling attracted and could tell she might be too. We sat in an area of the restaurant that overlooked the bar from a second story. When we sat down, we noticed about a dozen Asian women wearing bunny ears and sitting at a large table. Pretty soon we observed a man coming up the stairs, carrying a boom box and wearing a slick, satin-like police uniform. He was a male stripper there for the group of bunny-eared women having a bachelorette party, so we had some free entertainment.

Despite the distraction, Maripat and I continued to talk and find more similarities. I asked who her divorce attorney was, but she didn't want to tell me because "everybody hated her." Having switched attorneys just a couple of weeks earlier, I said, "Let me tell you mine and see where we go from there." It turned out we both had the same divorce attorney. We also discovered that both our mothers had passed away and were buried in the same cemetery about a hundred yards apart.

After dinner, we walked back to the hotel and said good night. Maripat told me later that she could not sleep that night; she knew something was going on that she did not understand. I invited her to join me for a buffet breakfast the next morning, so we met for breakfast. Our meal lasted a couple hours. We talked about a lot of things—

in essence, we were interviewing each other and being very cautious.

After having been on a few dates, we both asked many questions to learn about each other. Maripat asked me what I was looking for in a relationship. I told her I was looking for someone to share my life with and for shared goals and moral values. She said she was interested in finding someone whose shoulder she could finally put her head on and then take a deep breath. What she said scared me. I thought that she wanted someone to support her. That was exactly what I was trying to get away from.

She asked me if I missed checking in with someone while away, and I said yes. I explained that it was important for me to feel connected to someone, regardless of where I was because I need a home base.

After breakfast, we exchanged phone numbers and promised to keep in touch. Maripat finished her 40-hour layover in Hong Kong and returned to Chicago the next day. I went to work out after breakfast and then flew on to Singapore that evening. I returned to Chicago two days after Maripat.

With only three days off, I spent them training hard at the gym and skating, and then I flew a three-day Shanghai trip. Then off for two days, training hard at the gym again, followed by a three-day Beijing trip.

It was two weeks before I could call her. Maripat was used to having men call her right away, so she was very perplexed when I did not. A friend of hers told her to take the chance, so she called me instead.

I am very glad she did. She wanted to have coffee, so we met in Barrington. We spent 4 hours together. Walking around the quaint village, we talked nonstop, sharing our past and hopes for the future. I definitely felt energized by her beauty, her charm, her presence.

Working up the courage to revisit the statement that had bothered me, I asked what she meant when she said she wanted someone whose shoulder she could put her head on. I was looking through my filter to a failed marriage, so I saw a completely different picture of what she said. Hearing those words, I envisioned a woman who would lean on me and expect me to be strong and willing to sacrifice myself for her. When Maripat answered, I was glad that I had asked her to clarify. What she meant was finding someone with whom she could be vulnerable and her true self, without having to maintain a pretense.

What a sense of relief her answer gave me. Now that the air was cleared, I felt much more at ease. We truly enjoyed each other's company and clearly wanted to spend more time together. When we parted company, we promised again to keep in touch.

Although I was apprehensive about getting into another relationship, and I still had old wounds from my marriage to recognize, deal with, and heal, I knew enough to not get in my own way. As I allowed the relationship to unfold at its own pace without force, I knew deep down that something good was happening. Not knowing the result yet, I still trusted that the outcome would be right. Sometimes we need to have faith, and this was one of those times.

Sometimes, events and relationships have a rightness that you can't explain. With Maripat, I had that kind of feeling, so I decided to go with it. We experienced so many coincidences, or were they signs? Some force was at work, bringing us together at this time for a reason.

Wanting to create a relationship that would feed my soul, I knew deep down that I needed some tools to be able to start the process. More than six years into our relationship and marriage, I know now that my instincts were right. I have grown a great deal with Maripat. With a rough idea of what kind of relationship I wanted, I put what I was looking for out to the universe and I have since grown into it. Most importantly, however, we have healed some very old wounds.

Maripat has also done some deep work and found some very deep healing. She has said that I have been able to provide for her a safe place for her to heal. She has done the same for me as well.

We met again for coffee about a week after that pivotal conversation. Maripat had an appointment and was pressed for time. Letting her go, I wanted to talk more and learn all I could, but it was not to be that day.

A couple days later, she called and wanted to do something fun. I said yes. The leaves were turning, and Maripat wanted to go for a drive in the country. I have always felt a spiritual connection with nature. To walk in the woods is a great way for me to get closer to myself, and I wanted to share that with her. I know a place in Wisconsin about an hour and half north of my home that is a great place to hike. Maripat suggested a place called Palmyra, but I said "No, let's go to Kettle Moraine." I asked if she might come to my house and we could leave from there.

On a Sunday morning, she came over. As we drove north through the country, we talked nonstop again. Close to Kettle Moraine there was a sign for Palmyra. I realized then that the southern end of the same area, mostly devoted to horse trails, was called Palmyra. The northern end of the area, used for hiking and mountain biking, was called Kettle Moraine. We had been speaking of the same place but calling it by different names. We were both, without realizing it, drawn to the same place. This was another synchronous event that shaped our lives, our story, and our relationship. After a great two-hour hike in the woods, we drove to get something to eat. It was then that we broke down the barriers by enjoying our first kiss and the start of an amazing relationship.

A few days later, I fell while skating. The blade of my right skate cut the inside of my left ankle, resulting in seven stitches and a sprained ankle. This occurred at the peak of work in my skating season, so I was distraught. Generally at the end of October, skaters put in a lot of volume and intensity before we start to taper off so we won't be overtrained for racing. I worried that a couple of weeks off would affect my racing for the year, which was still greatly tied up with my self-worth as measured by my skating performance.

If I missed workouts, that might affect my speed. Everything had to be perfect or I could not achieve my best effort. This injury was a fly in the ointment, and I needed help to deal with it. Knowing that Maripat was a caretaker, I called her. I was hurt and vulnerable. Baring my soul to her, I confessed that I allowed my self-worth to be defined by my achievements. If I could not achieve, then who was I? It was a tough time for me. My honesty about what I was going through gave us the perfect opportunity to see what we were both made of.

Asking for help was tough, but worth the risk. It just felt right. Maripat came over right away. I lay on the sofa with my stitched, swollen, and sprained ankle elevated and the fear of not being good enough weighing me down. Hurt emotionally and physically, and just plain scared. Maripat understood completely. Opening up to her that day was a watershed moment for me.

This is where I started to recognize what was happening to me. Because of my circumstances I began making better choices and laying the groundwork for future events. When things seemingly beyond my control suddenly fell into place, I realized that I could achieve almost anything. By doing the work and setting the stage for a positive outcome, good things would come my way in time. With a newfound gratitude, I continued the internal and external work on myself, trusting that there was a plan for me. This reinforced my concept that hard work, trust, and patience would lead to a better place for me and those close to me.

Maripat was also looking for a relationship in which she could experience trust and could heal from her past wounds. Finding a safe place and the ability to come to me with the same vulnerability allowed her to know that healing could take place. A couple of months later, she moved in with me, and we began to share a house together. We were married on September 17, 2011, in Gold Hill, Colorado, on a cliff overlooking the continental divide. Our union has brought out our true selves. At first, a new relationship can be frightening, but trusting that we were meant to be together is comforting. The barriers that separate us from each other as well as from our authentic selves are the key. Breaking through our limiting beliefs will reveal the true treasures we all seek in our relationships with ourselves and our loved ones.

CHAPTER WISDOM

Ask the universe for what you need. Keep moving, and trust that whatever comes your way is in your best interest.

PART TWO

PART TWO

CHAPTER 6

BREAKING DOWN BARRIERS I: AN EXAMPLE FROM SKATING

There is great wisdom in breaking down barriers to maximize personal possibilities. The process is simple but not easy. First, identify what works. Second, define the barriers to progress. Finally, use what brings you success to overcome your barriers.

Barriers to progress come in many different forms. The first type is the external barrier. An example from my life is when a doctor told me that, because I did not have perfect vision, I would never be an airline pilot. This limitation was a perceived external barrier. Had I chosen to accept it, I would have internalized it and never become an airline pilot.

The second type is the internal barrier. For example, I might love to play basketball. If I am shorter than other players around me, I could say to myself that my height means I will never be competitive and should give up. However, plenty of shorter players love to play and excel at the game regardless of their height. My negative belief would be an internal barrier.

Some barriers might be unconscious. For example, if my third-grade teacher told me I was not good at math, I might have internalized that thought so deeply that I no longer remember the original statement. Yet, it could still control me and cause me to avoid math for the rest of my life and pursue things that don't require it.

Barriers may be conscious, cultural, hereditary, regional, rooted in history, or rooted in a person's past. The key to pushing past the restrictive beliefs we have, the thoughts that become our barriers to achievement, is not to limit the concept of success. By taking responsibility for success, then expanding your concepts, you naturally break down barriers to goals. Give yourself permission to be great. We have a lot more capability than we give ourselves credit for.

Here is an example of the tangible result of breaking down my own barriers. On December 3, 2005, I achieved a qualifying time to compete in the Olympic trials for the 2006 Winter Olympic Games. The trials were held just after Christmas at the indoor oval in Salt Lake City. Six weeks later in February 2006, the Games would be held in Torino, Italy. The last time I competed in the Olympic trials I was 19 years old. I had a real chance to make the team. In 2005, I was 49 years old and had no chance to earn one of the top five spots to go to Torino. My goals had changed over the last 30 years. This time my goal was simply to compete at an elite level once again.

This first barrier to overcome was the inner barrier of the age-limiting belief about "getting slower as we get older." The next barrier was the external fact that I had been away from speed skating for 22 years. Another internal barrier was my tendency to go overboard with my training. I exhibited this principle as a youth by not allowing a coach to tell me to slow down; thus, I overtrained. The final barrier was my need to prove to myself that I was good enough. I had reconciled myself to the idea that I would never be an Olympian, but could I skate fast enough to get back to this elite level as a 49-year-old "masters" skater? If I could do something no one else was doing, would that be good enough for me?

To deal with the age-limiting belief, I needed only to listen to myself. By taking one step at a time, I could make continuous progress. By blocking out all the noise, I could focus on the task at hand. I keep very specific records of my training. Progress can be measured and thus expected every day.

Skating had changed a great deal while I was gone from the sport. Since the landscape was very different, I could take a fresh look at skating and my relation to it. I would have to adapt to new technology like the new clap skate; that necessity made change easier.

My tendency to overtrain could be held in check by having a coach to trust and rely upon. By being honest with myself and my coach, I could learn from and avoid my past mistakes.

The last barrier was the need to prove to myself that I could still be an elite skater. I made a list of affirmations and read them frequently to reinforce the concept of doing the work and trusting the results, both external and internal. I shared the affirmations with the people I was closest to for the external support I sometimes needed.

The story of the Olympic trials, December 26th, 2005, Salt Lake City, Utah, illustrates one result of all this work.

When I arrived at the rink the day before racing, I needed to do a little skating to get the feel of the ice. I checked in at the front desk. The rink had already been closed to the public, and the media was restricted from going into the locker rooms inside the oval.

Only competitors in the trials were allowed on the ice now. I needed an ID tag to get to the ice and the locker rooms reserved for the skaters. When the attendant at the desk asked me if I was checking in as coach, I said, "No, a skater." Her question really caught me off guard. At that stage in my life, I guess I did look more like a coach than an athlete. She looked me up on the list and handed me the athlete badge I had earned. When people look at me, they might see a coach. What I feel on the inside is an athlete of 26. I walked away from that desk with a new sense of pride in what I was accomplishing, a part of something much bigger than myself.

Thirty years after my first Olympic trials, I was skating faster than ever. Wow, what a difference it made to have a coach and to do things differently. I was overwhelmed with emotion and at the same time a deep sense of peace. I was feeling my mother very close and how proud she was of me, even though she had passed away almost 6 years before. I had earned a spot among my peers of elite skaters. Some of them were younger than my own children, yet I belonged there. I was home. All that had gone on before and all that had happened to get me there were supporting me in that moment. I was honored to be among such talented athletes.

Gliding around the 400-meter indoor oval in Salt Lake City was like floating on air, like having an out-of-body experience. I was accompanied on the ice by my skating tribe, my family of fellow skaters. We were not competitors in the sense of normal competition. I was there just to take part, not to compete for a spot on the Olympic team.

Honored to participate, I felt good to be among my peers and to have earned my place there like anyone else. I was about to do the on-ice warm-up for the racing later. The family and friends of all the skaters filled the stands. The air was warm, about 60 degrees. No gloves or hats could be seen in the Salt Lake indoor oval; the air was warm enough to skate with bare hands and head. The ice was fantastic, smooth and fast. The electricity in the building was palpable. With a spring in my step, I felt almost invincible. I had been tapering down my workouts leading up to this moment, so my fast twitch muscle fibers would be able to fire when ready, to sprint at maximum effort. I imagined the wind rushing by my ears when I did a 200-meter acceleration, and I put on my protective glasses. Without them, my eyes would water from the 35-mph wind in my face, and I would not be able to see. Time to settle in and get focused on the task at hand. This was the work that I love to do so dearly, work that I am meant do in this lifetime.

I had bought airline tickets for my kids, my wife (even though she and I were separated), and me to travel late on Christmas Day to Salt Lake. Considering it was the trip of a lifetime for my family and me, the expense was worth it. My father would be flying up from Oklahoma City to meet us as well.

I would race the 500-meter race twice on December 27, about two hours apart. Then the 1000-meter race the next day. I could also skate the 1000 again a few days later, but I declined that opportunity so I could spend a couple of days skiing with my kids in the Utah Mountains.

My normal routine for a race day has changed over the years. I have been able, with the help of my coach, to find what works for me and refine it to a carefully planned and orchestrated ritual. The months leading up to this moment were very well planned. It also allowed for some adjustments to cover the unforeseen obstacles that might pop up in the course of life. Starting the night before, I sharpened my skates, then I checked all the gear necessary for the next day's racing.

I like to arrive at the rink an hour before getting on the ice. My pre-race routine includes cycling on a stationary bike, dynamic stretching (using motion to gradually stretch muscles to their maximum range), static stretching (stretching muscles while the body is at rest), imitation skating on dry land, and then finally changing into my skin suit. I eat a banana while carrying my skate bag through the tunnel under the ice to the inside of the oval. I get on the ice for about 25 minutes, a few easy laps and a series of progressively faster and shorter distances. During this process in Salt Lake, I felt a sense of awe. Deep in thought and concentration at times, focused on the task, I blocked out the world. Pausing to reflect on what was happening on a bigger scale was very important.

The intangibles that had placed me there were what I was feeling. With a true sense of what was going on inside and outside of me, I was overwhelmed with emotion. I was proud of what I had accomplished and grateful for where I was and my path to this point.

I finished my ice warm-up with some starts from a standing position. Visualizing my racing the entire time, focusing on being in the moment stroke by stroke. Rehearsing starter's commands and exploding off the starting line. From the draw the previous evening, I knew the lane to start from. I pictured the start, first turn, the backstretch and the crossover, the second turn, and the final straight and finish.

Then I stepped off the ice, took off my skates, and rested before the next pre-race warm-up phase. The pre-race routine warmed up the muscles and nervous system, creating a little lactic acid buildup. As a result, I had to recover with a little rest to be able to fire on all cylinders. I found a quiet place, lay on the floor, and put my legs up on a wall to help the process. After that, I did a few minutes of stationary bike to get a sweat going again before getting onto the ice. Once on the ice, I did a few easy laps, practiced a few starts, then approached the starting line, all while conserving my energy. It is a real art to make it to the starting line in just the right physical, mental, emotional, and spiritual condition.

The women raced first. After a short break to resurface the ice, the men started. I felt flexible from the static and dynamic stretching, mentally alert but not nervous, calm and collected but ready to spring when the gun went off for the start.

I was slated to be the second of about fifteen pairs of skaters. Racing is set up so the fastest skaters are last. This was my chance to display what I had. My goals had changed from 1975; this time I was not a contender for the team but a participant. The other skater in my pair was Mitchell Whitmore from Kalamazoo, Michigan. He was 17.

With a solid start, I stayed pretty close to Mitch through the first 100 meters and the first turn. We crossed over on the backstretch and skated the last turn. He finished just a few feet ahead. Looking up, I saw that I had skated the second-fastest 500 ever for me, 39.51. About an hour later, I skated another 500 from the opposite starting lane. I was paired with Mitch again. Again he beat me by a few feet. This time I skated even faster—38.95! My fastest 500 ever and a sub 39! I was overjoyed.

At that competition, NBC took a special interest in my story. My brother Bart had put out a press release for me about three weeks earlier when I qualified for the trials. Having a younger brother as an Olympic Champion and a television analyst lent great credibility to my story when it broke. During my racing that day, a film crew followed me around. They took video of my warm-up routine, skating, and racing. They videoed and interviewed my family, coach, and fellow competitors.

After the day's racing was over, they asked to interview me. I drove to the east side of Salt Lake City to a producer's home for the filming. A reporter from Los Angeles asked me questions over a speakerphone, and I answered by speaking and looking into a camera. I was floored that the media took such an interest in me and my story. Even so, I was not quite ready to talk about the experience in larger terms yet; I was still processing the event and the different layers, physical, mental, and emotional. Although I was certainly pleased with the attention, I could not claim to be the oldest competitor there. Boris Leikin, a Russian-born naturalized citizen, was racing too. Boris was 3-1/2 years older than me and going almost as fast.

The interview was broadcast the next morning on the *Today Show* and introduced by Matt Lauer. Matt is about a year younger than me, and he was astounded that I could do such a thing. You can see this *Today Show* story on my website, at www.brucewconner.com. The next day I raced the 1000 meters, and *Today* did a follow-up story as well. I believe that they did a great job in explaining that I viewed these trials as my personal Olympics.

Since I will never be an Olympian, I must be realistic. I can still experience the feeling of being a champion, enjoy the journey, and celebrate what I have done. It is nice to have the outward recognition and notoriety. What is far more important is how I interpret the events, how I take them in and feed my own self esteem. This experience has helped fuel me to more and greater things. It has helped me break down additional barriers in my own thinking. It has shown my children and anyone who cares to listen what can be accomplished through this process. Most of my limitations are between my own ears. Change my thinking and I change my life. Celebrating this event as my Olympics is a concrete example of the tangible results of what I do.

By taking these steps I have also healed some very deep wounds to my self-esteem. The work, the journey, and the results have helped to make me whole as never before.

CHAPTER WISDOM

By breaking down barriers, we can show ourselves and the world that we are more capable than we give ourselves credit for.

CHAPTER 7

BREAKING DOWN BARRIERS II: AN EXAMPLE FROM PILOTING

Another example of breaking down barriers comes from my flying career. The goal of my flying career was to get hired by a major airline such as United, Delta, or American as soon as possible. The date you are hired determines your seniority and thus your rank (captain, first officer, flight engineer), pay, type of airplanes, routes, and time off. To get hired, you must compete with other professional pilots for the spots available at each airline. To be competitive means to be the best, most qualified applicant for the job. The major factors in being competitive are having a college degree, your flight time (the type of time you have is very important—larger, more complex airplanes are better), your technical ability, etc. The airlines will also look at many other intangibles such as personality; communication skills; health; a history of being a stable, good employee; and the intangible quality of being someone they would trust to fly their family.

The barriers to progress were the fact that I did not have perfect vision, I had no military training, I was competing with many pilots for few jobs, the industry had low starting pay, and pilots needed to relocate to where the jobs were.

In high school, I was recruited for a position at the Air Force Academy in Colorado Springs. When I spoke to the recruiter, he told me I would never fly for the Air Force due to my imperfect vision. So many applicants had perfect vision, they did not want to deal with anyone who did not have it. My vision was 20/40. I required glasses to have 20/20. All the military programs required perfect vision. So I decided that the military was not the way to go. After doing some research, I learned that not all the airlines required perfect vision, so I still had a chance to be a major airline pilot.

As I mentioned earlier, my father and I found a school in Kenosha, Wisconsin, where I could get an associate's degree and learn how to fly. It was located halfway to the rink in Milwaukee, so I could continue to train for the next Olympic team. I went to school and learned to fly from August 1974 till June 1977, taking all the requisite courses for flying, as well as the general education courses for an associate's degree. I passed the written, oral, and practical tests for private, commercial, instrument, multiengine, flight instructor, instrument instructor, instrument and advanced ground instructor's certificates.

Living at home in Morton Grove, Illinois, for all except one semester kept my costs down. I did rent a room in a Kenosha family's basement for one semester when I was taking 21 credit hours and working on my instrument rating. I did take one fall semester off (1975) school to train in the Netherlands for the upcoming 1976 Olympic games.

After graduation, I sent out a couple hundred resumes. Pilots were a dime a dozen then. I received one response from a fixed-based operator looking for a freelance flight instructor. I drove to Waunakee, Wisconsin, just northwest of Madison for the interview. Dan Bindl, the owner, liked me and offered me the position. He had a home on a 2,300-foot long, grass runway. The east 1,000 feet were paved and about 25 feet wide. The runway was pretty nice for teaching people who did not want to drive down to the big airport in Madison. I started there in June 1977. The owner had an eight-sided house that had a hangar on the bottom floor. Bordering the runway were about 30 other homes, mostly owned by people who had airplanes. I was pretty busy through the summer and early fall. I had a cot above one of the hangar areas.

In October, I learned that they did not plan to keep the runway plowed through the winter. Being a freelance instructor, I would loose my income-earning capability. I had just rented a house in town for my new fiancé and me. I went down to Palwaukee Airport in a northwest suburb of Chicago and was able to secure a flight instructor position at Priester Aviation very quickly. Moving back to the Chicago area, I started my new job and got married all in the same week. That was October 1977. I stayed at Priester till January 1979. In this instance, the external barrier of learning that my income-earning potential would not last forced me to move fast and find a steadier job.

At Priester, I mostly taught people who wanted the private-pilot certificate. I also taught commercial and instrument flying. Later, I added a multiengine instructor certificate, so I could instruct people how to fly multiengine airplanes. By January 1979, I had a couple thousand hours of flight time, most of which was as an instructor. I also attended a Lear Jet ground school so I could be a co-pilot in Lear Jets.

The only real long-term, secure jobs were with the major airlines. Everything else was a stepping-stone. After the deregulation of the airlines in 1978, the major airlines had been hiring a high number of pilots. I was pretty well qualified by then but not good enough. I knew some people in the business and talked to them about my chances of getting hired. The oil embargo of 1979 slowed down the boom, and the controllers' strike in 1980 also caused problems. The whole industry came to a screeching halt. At one point in 1979, United Airlines went from hiring one day to laying guys off the next day before they even came to school for training. There were a lot of decent jobs out there, but I was only interested in the major carriers. I wanted to fly big airplanes to faraway places, to see passengers in the terminal reuniting with loved ones, to be part of the process of people getting together.

I knew that to get the best seniority, I needed to be as competitive as possible when the hiring cycle started again so I would be one of the first ones hired. Teaching six days a week, 12-hour days, I had burned out as a flight instructor. Instructing close to the maximum allowable number of 8 hours every day is great for building experience and time, but it's exhausting. Fortunately for me, the commuter airlines were hiring and expanding when the major airlines were scaling back.

I knew it would be good to have some airline experience next. My next job was flying Beech 18's in Rolla, Missouri, for Skyway Aviation.

PART TWO

It was a passenger commuter airline. My wife and I packed up our apartment full of stuff and moved south to Rolla so I could start my first airline job—captain of a nine-passenger, piston-engine, propeller-driven, tailwheel commuter airplane.

When I was hired, I had little experience in tailwheel airplanes, which can be very tricky to taxi, takeoff, and land. After two weeks in the right seat as a copilot, I checked out as a captain. I received my airline transport pilot's certificate in a Beech 18. About thirty pilots and co-pilots worked at this small company. We had no autopilots or radar. We managed as best we could and tried to keep on schedule. Sometimes we would fly sixteen legs in one day at 180 miles per hour. We had four Beech 18's that were as old as I was, twenty-three. We also had three DC-3s, which is a slightly larger plane that seats nineteen. This was also a twin-engine, piston-driven airplane. We mostly flew to small towns in Missouri from the two hubs in St Louis and Kanas City.

We all survived, and as far I know, we are all flying for the major air carriers now. The commuter airline was having some financial trouble a few months after I started. I was scared that we would go out of business and I would be out of work. After sending out some more resumes, I happened to meet Ron Puffer, a friend and fellow Skyway pilot, at another commuter airline. We met outside the office of the chief pilot of Scheduled Skyways, in Fayetteville, Arkansas. Ron had a scheduled interview. When he introduced himself to the chief pilot, I did the same. The chief pilot asked if I had a current resume. I said yes and handed it to him. He asked me to come in and sit down with Ron.

Once we were in the office, he said that my name sounded familiar. Then he looked down on his desk to see a resume that I had sent him a week earlier. In fact, he said, he had been planning to call me. The three of us talked for a while, and he offered us both jobs on the spot. As this shows, planning, persistence, and networking paid off.

I took the job and started two weeks later. They had two kinds of turboprop airplanes. They had been flying Beech 99's, and they were expanding with Swearingen Metroliners. The Beech 99's were fifteen-seat unpressurized turboprops, and the Metroliners were nineteen-seat and had pressurized cabins. By regulation, the most passenger capacity you could have without a flight attendant is nineteen seats. The airplanes had airborne weather radars but no autopilots.

We flew to many major hubs, including Kansas City, Dallas, Memphis, and St Louis. We covered many south and south-central states. Flying a turboprop was the best way to get quality time to be competitive when the major carriers started hiring again. I built time as a copilot in both airplanes.

In about a year and a half, I made captain. We were flying about 100-120 hours a month, which is a lot more than major airlines fly because the rules are different.

The company also had a flight school and a charter business. Because I had experience in a Cessna 310—a six-seat, twin-engine airplane from my time at Priester Aviation in the Chicago area—I flew a little charter work, and I trained other pilots on the Cessna 310. The chief pilot asked if I wanted to be chief flight instructor of the flight school. Knowing it would look good on my resume, I agreed.

Five flight instructors were teaching there then. The local FAA office needed someone to be a designated examiner to test for private, commercial, instrument, and multiengine certificates. An FAA official in Little Rock had given me a check ride and liked the way I worked, so he asked me if I wanted to be the FAA Designated Examiner in northwest Arkansas, meaning that people would come to me get their ratings and certificates. I said yes!

After training in Oklahoma City for a week, I became probably the youngest-ever examiner at age 24. Such an achievement would look good on my resume too.

In 1983, the major airlines started to hire again. My brother Bart was living in Norman, Oklahoma, and commuting to Las Vegas to see his physical therapist for lingering, sports-related injuries. He had developed a relationship with a small airline called Sunworld. They had four DC-9-10's. This was a ninety-seat jet, just like the major airlines used. Sunworld was hiring and expanding. Bart helped me get in the door for an interview; the rest would be up to me. They hired me to be a copilot on a jet! My network and persistence had paid off again.

I started in March 1984. After I completed initial training at Sunworld, my wife and I packed up all our worldly belongings and moved to Las Vegas.

I was now going to get some jet time at last. With that on my resume, I determined to be as aggressive about pursuing my goal of flying for a major carrier as I could be. Eastern, Delta, Northwest, and American were all starting to hire. I applied to all of them, knowing that some would throw my application in the trash because of my imperfect vision. For example, I interviewed with American in June 1984. They turned me down for vision even though they had announced that they were dropping the requirement for perfect vision in a couple of weeks. They said, "Sorry, apply again in six months."

In contrast, United called me in September for an initial interview and testing. I went to Chicago for the first phase, then to Denver for the next phase of flying a simulator, a physical exam, and another interview. I remember flying home to Las Vegas first class in a DC-10 on a United company pass. After takeoff, I got very emotional. I had done everything I needed to do for the job, and the rest was up to United and out of my hands. All I could do was wait on the results. A couple of weeks later, a mailgram arrived saying that I got the job! I had won the pilot's lottery—flying jets for a major airline.

United was just starting to hire again after they had recalled all of the pilots they furloughed in 1979. I was offered a training slot on January 29, 1985. My wife was pregnant with our son and due after I was scheduled to finish training. She ended up having an emergency C-section, and our son was born 5-1/2 weeks early.

A week later, I was in Denver for training as a flight engineer on the Boeing 727, the traditional starting spot for new hires. I was hired along with 569 other pilots (later known as the 570) and offered a training spot that would determine my seniority. The training lasted 20 days. I finished with a flight engineer turbojet certificate. I got one day off in the middle of training, so I went home to Las Vegas to see my wife and new son.

When I told Sunworld that I had to go to this training, they said they understood what I had to do for my career. I was next in line at Sunworld to upgrade to DC-9 Captain. They told me that they would not upgrade me to captain, but if I came back after training, they would keep me as a copilot for long as it took to replace me or until United offered me employment.

Unfortunately, things did not go very smoothly after that. Another barrier to my plan cropped up.

The pilots' union at United was trying to negotiate a new contract. The company had hired us 570 pilots before a possible work stoppage, trained us, and then sent us home pending a new contract with the union. When I returned to Sunworld in February, I found out that my employers had changed their mind. Sunworld was afraid that other pilots would do the same thing of remaining on their payroll while preparing to leave the company. In short, I was no longer employed.

I was now out of work, responsible for a new son, and unsure what would happen with United. I interviewed with a couple of companies for flying positions during the spring of 1985. I flew to San Diego to interview with Pacific Southwest Airlines. I was honest with them about my pending situation with United and what had happened with Sunworld. They said thanks for coming and terminated the interview pretty quickly.

In the meantime, I packed up all our belongings and put them in storage in Las Vegas. I put my son and wife on a Sunworld airplane to fly to Oklahoma City. I packed up the families' 1966 Pontiac Catalina, put my two Labrador retrievers in it, and pulled a trailer with the essential stuff we needed to live with relatives for the next year. We moved in with my parents in Norman, Oklahoma, where my father was a professor at the University of Oklahoma. We moved into an upstairs bedroom next to my newborn son in another room. The strike came on May 17th. I honored the picket line, as did 95 percent of the line pilots and the group of 570. The strike ended 29 days later.

United reneged on their agreement with the 570 and refused to offer us employment even though they now had a new contract. The union stood by us, but we had to take the company to court. The federal judge in Chicago ordered United to hire us—but only after all the pilots that had been hired to replace us during the strike were trained. My wife, new son, and I bounced around from Oklahoma to Chicago, from relative to relative, till United sent me a mailgram in November 1985 asking me to show up for my final phase of training in early December. We moved back to the Chicago suburbs and by the time I started flying again, I had been out of work for 10-1/2 months. The union paid me as though I had been flying since the end of the strike in mid-June. Although that amounted to only about the same amount I had been paid as a commuter turboprop captain in 1980, it kept us from going bankrupt. Now I had a much more secure future and pretty good seniority.

The hard work in getting hired by United as soon as possible paid off. I can say that my position now as a 747 captain is the result of all that happened before. It has not been very smooth sailing at United. The original court case that awarded our jobs back after the strike was reversed in the appellate court, then appealed to the Supreme Court, where the case was not heard. As a result, it stood as being overturned.

The company could terminate us anytime it wanted after that decision in 1988. The union negotiated a deal to keep our jobs, but we had to go behind all those that had been hired during and immediately after the strike. My seniority rank dropped by 539 places in an instant. It took a new contract and 5-1/2 years to get our original, rightful seniority back to the date we first showed up for work.

I moved up in my first, probationary year at United to first officer on the 727. During that year, I bid for and was awarded a spot on the 727 as a copilot. I worried a little about going back to training during my probationary year. If I did not do well in training, the company could fire me with little recourse. Because I had flown jets before United, I figured that if I did not have confidence in my abilities by then, maybe I should not be flying for a living.

I dove in headfirst. Training went great, and I was at the flying controls again instead of watching the guys and gals up front doing the flying while I did the paperwork, made the passenger announcements, and managed the fuel, electrics, hydraulics, pressurization, and air conditioning. During my career at United, I have steadily progressed up to larger and more sophisticated airplanes. I made Boeing 747-400 captain in 2003.

I have made it to the top of my field by breaking down the barriers to progress. If I had stopped anywhere along the line, I would have failed. I chose not to stop. That is one way to success. Keep pressing on. Keep finding ways to make progress despite what happens. When I came upon blocks to progress, I tried to see if they were internal or external. If they were internal, then I needed to change my mind to see other solutions. If they were external, then I needed to see if I could get around them or change course entirely. I also learned to accept things that were beyond my control.

The next chapter deals with the methods to recognizing and dealing with all kinds of barriers and limiting beliefs.

CHAPTER WISDOM

Keep moving in the direction of your goals, adjust as necessary to meet the present circumstances, accept what you cannot control, and trust that you are on the right path.

PART TWO

CHAPTER 8

HOW TO BREAK DOWN LIMITING BELIEFS AND OTHER BARRIERS

What kind of barriers do you have? What kind of barriers do you want to get rid of? What will be the benefit of getting rid of those barriers? What will be the potential cost of getting rid of those barriers? Are there any possible unintended consequences? These are all questions we must ask of ourselves. By defining our blocks to progress, we clearly see our barriers.

Many times, I look at my barriers and see that they are not just keeping me from doing something, but they are also protecting me from potential pain. What am I afraid of? If I break through a barrier, I will be accountable and responsible for where I am. Am I ready for that? Am I ready to take on that responsibility?

Doing this work takes a lot of courage. Am I ready to exercise my courage? I always thought that courage was doing big heroic deeds. Now, I see courage as saying, "YES!" in difficult situations. It is taking the small steps every day, then looking up after a while to see how far I have come. Those small steps were not hard at the time, yet when I look at the big picture, I see that I have achieved a lot.

We all have our issues. We are all unique. Yet, we probably have more things in common than we think. We can share in this journey through life and know we are not alone. I want to be peaceful, happy, joyous, and free. I want to be able to make my own decisions and live my life the way I want, the way I see as the best way for me. This philosophy of thinking helps me do that.

How do I determine if there is a barrier? That can be pretty easy. Look at the areas where you are not moving forward. Where do you want to go? What is holding you back? For example, if I am having difficulty with my financial situation, then I need to look at my relationship with money and the preconceived ideas I have about money. I need to be as honest with myself as possible. The more honest I can be, the clearer the picture will be and the easier it will be to break down my own barriers.

Periodically, I sit down with a trusted friend to share where I am having trouble in my life. This helps me to see what barriers I am creating for myself and what I am really fighting. After identifying my barriers, I can determine what to do about them.

Ignore them, go around them, or just bust through. Sometimes all I have to do is change my mind about something. This might sound overly simplistic, but it works. The process for breaking down barriers involves three steps: awareness, acceptance, and action.

Awareness is the first big step in this process. Once I figure out what the barrier is, I can figure out what to do about it. Is it internal or external? If it is external, I need to know all I can about it before I tackle it. Are there any holes in it? What does the landscape really look like? Is it a hard and fast barrier? Is it dependent on some person or institution to remain in place? Is it moveable? Will it go away with time?

If the barrier is internal, then what preconceived ideas are tied to the barrier? In other words, what ideas do I need to change? Can I accept those changes? What are the costs to changing my ideas? What changes am I willing to make? What am I not willing to budge on?

I have built a foundation on which I stand. This foundation has many blocks in it. If I am having trouble with a barrier, then maybe I need to do some digging. If my barrier has a foundation, then I must see how that foundation is built. I must be honest about what is keeping me from moving forward. Transformation usually is born out of a crisis or a sense of urgency. Getting around a barrier can be very tough. I have done a great deal in my life so far. This kind of work—of confronting internal barriers—is the hardest I have ever done, but it is the most valuable work by far. It unlocks the door to unlimited possibilities.

Most people will not undergo fundamental change unless they have no other choice. I needed to make some fundamental changes in the way I behaved to survive. I have found that because I made those fundamental changes, then I can apply these new ideas of change to other parts of my life. Once I learned the application to other areas of my life, it became easier and more universal.

Growing up in my family, I was blessed with parents who had open minds. First, we had clear goals. Then we had a plan to get there. We realized that we had to be flexible about that plan. With that in mind, I remember that whenever I asked my parents for something like extra coaching or better skates, they would say, "Let's find a way to make it happen." I would rarely hear no.

This set up a framework of looking at the goal first and keeping it the highest priority. Then when a barrier to progress came up, we would automatically try to figure out a way around it, over it, or through it. Sometimes we would figure out that the original path we were taking was not going to yield results and that maybe the obstacle was telling us to go a different way. This is where we had to be able to change our plans along the way.

Now, as an adult, I can see and break down barriers to all sorts of issues. Thereby, I enhance all parts of my life. I can be the person I am supposed to be without any roadblocks—not doing this to achieve more, but to be happy about who I am. It does translate into measurable achievement, but that is only a symptom and a byproduct of this work breaking down barriers.

Albert Einstein said, " Imagination is more important than knowledge." I believe Einstein is correct. I need to summon and nurse my imagination to create solutions. Then I must use my willpower to carry it out. It is also important to have a positive vision for the future. I have a picture on my computer that is my normal background for my desktop. It is a picture of me skating. The computer slightly stretched it to fit the screen, which distorted my position and makes me look better than I really am. It shows me built better (larger muscles), it shows me in a lower skating position, and it shows me with more lean in the turn. I love this photo because it shows me what I am working on. It is a positive view for me, and I aspire to being the guy skating in the image. My attitude about this photo is a positive one that I choose, making the decisions to do the work to be that guy. Positive, realistic images are that ones that inspire me. What about you? I believe that long-term, positive reinforcement will outlast negative fear-based motivation every time.

When you face a big project ahead, it can look very daunting. By breaking it down into pieces, it becomes more manageable. Once I do that, I just take things step by step, making small progress day by day. Great big accomplishments do not happen overnight but take time and many steps.

I also need to ask myself about owning my own power. Too frequently I have given away my power and given it in too many forms. I am more powerful than I give myself credit for. If I am waiting for permission, then I have already given my power away. If you need permission from someone, then take it from me, say yes, and "Do it!" Owning your own power can be exhilarating! It can also be quite scary. Once you get the hang of it, nothing will stop you.

I am not talking about running roughshod over others, quite the contrary. What I am talking about is about a core self-esteem that says, "I am worth fighting for. I value myself first. I feel best when I can help others." What is important about this concept is that by taking care of myself first, then I can be of service to others. The flight attendants' briefing about the use of the oxygen mask before each flight demonstrates this. If I put on my mask first, I can help those around me. If I do not take care of myself first, then I will pass out from lack of oxygen and am of no use to anyone.

Another example I love to use is our own circulation system. Our hearts pump continuously, selflessly for our very survival. We don't ask it to; our heart just pumps. Once the blood comes back from the body, it goes through the heart. The next place it goes after that is to the lungs to get re-oxygenated. Then the blood goes directly back to feed the heart muscle itself. It does not go to the body first; the heart takes care of itself first. Then the blood goes out to other parts of the body. The lesson here is that I must take care of myself first before I can help anyone else. If I do not do that, I will get burned up and not be able to help anyone, including myself.

The next step in the process of breaking down barriers is acceptance. I do not have to like something in order to accept it. It took me a long time to understand that concept. It is certainly easier to accept something if I like it, but it's not necessary. To me, acceptance means that I accept things just the way they are right now. I cannot have any judgment about this part of acceptance. Once I can accept, then I can see more clearly what is to be done. Then I can make a new decision about how to move forward.

In the fall of 2001, about a year and a half after my mother's death, I was still having a tough time accepting that she was gone. She was an exceptional woman, and I felt a need to carry on her legacy somehow. I fought with the idea of acceptance. I thought I had to like the situation to accept it. Quite the contrary.

First I had to stop fighting and be okay with the facts as they were. She was gone and there was nothing I could do about it. Then I had to move forward with a new vision. I was running in my neighborhood, and I know exactly when and where it happened. I came to the realization that I could not carry her message as she would, but I could add my experience to hers. Combining her memory with my knowledge and wisdom, I could carry on in a new way that would help me keep her close to me. This would provide some action to my healing, which leads me to the next step in the process.

The last step is action. First, I was aware, then I accepted, then I can act. Determining the right action can be daunting. I must take time to look at many options and weigh the costs and benefits. Then I must be okay with change and not look back. Buyer's remorse is a bad thing. I try to keep reinforcing the right decisions through "cognitive resonance." In this technique, I keep reinforcing the right decisions by finding more reasons to support the original decision.

Waiting is also an action. Sometimes the solution is still being worked out, and I need to wait for it. Another type of action is to ask for help. This can come from a number of different sources. In my life, I have certain experiences that are unique to me. My intelligence is limited. I need to access other sources of information and inspiration. I read a lot of books and draw from as many sources as possible when I need to make changes. If I can tap into other people's ideas, then I have a much greater chance of coming up with creative ways to look at my problems and find solutions.

I believe that we are all connected through a collective unconscious that I call God. I use God to help me change and grow. I have seen God work in my life as well as in those around me. I can tap into God and know I am being directed and put in the right place and the right time. By having faith and trusting that I am being led, I have peace that my path is right for me.

God speaks to me in a number of ways. My God speaks to me through other people, and he speaks to me internally. Usually, this comes in the form of inspiration and meditation. It is my job to be open to it all forms of input and to seek to learn when I can. In this way, I can get the direction I need.

I have seen miracles around me and have experienced them in my own life. I believe the right path in any situation is the one that connects my head to my heart and is open to a power greater than myself. I need to continue to trust that if I stay open to new possibilities, then I will continue on a path that is the right one for me.

This is a continual process. As I proceed, I can re-evaluate and make changes as I go. I need to be continually aware of where I am, what my goals are, and how I can proceed with breaking down my barriers.

So I have probably raised as many questions in this chapter as I have answered. Breaking down barriers is a tough issue. It can take many forms. It can also lead to many "ah-ha" moments. It is simple but not easy. I hope that I have raised your awareness of the problems with barriers and how to break them down so that you can move forward in whatever direction is right for you and your soul.

CHAPTER WISDOM

Define blocks to progress, figure out a way around them, set your goals, act, and trust the path ahead.

CHAPTER 9

MY FINAL SPEED SKATING BARRIER

My goals for the 2012-2013 skating season were to qualify for the upcoming U.S. Olympic Long Track Speed Skating Trials for the 2014 Winter Olympic Games. The trials were held in late December 2013. The skating season that would last from September 2012 through March 2013 would be when I could achieve the times necessary for each distance. According to the rules at that time, the 500-meter race required a time of 39.00 seconds or better. The 1000-meter race required a time of 1:16.08.

To try to achieve those times, I would skate some local time trial races in Milwaukee as well as some masters competitions in Milwaukee and Salt Lake.

I make a hundred or more decisions every day that affect my health, happiness, peace, and serenity. Even so, I do look for some external validation that I am on the right track. I am human. I can admit that.

One of the ways I get feedback is through my speed skating performance. Speed skating is a great mirror for my life. Physical preparation is essential. Physical execution is necessary too. Mental preparation is important for execution. I need to manage my emotional state to get the best results. I also need to trust in my spiritual life. Proper preparation gives me the deep-down trust that I am on the right track and that my priorities are right. I feel very strongly that I am doing what I was put on this earth to do.

On a September Saturday morning, I arose at 4:00 am. I drove 75 miles to Milwaukee to start my pre-race, off-ice warm up at 6:45. On-ice warm up is from 7:30 to 8:00 am. Racing starts at 8:30. I was in the eleventh pair of the 500-meter race. I had the inner lane with Brandon Molenda (14 years old) in the outer lane. After a clean start, he was in front for about the first 30 meters. I was able to get low, lengthen my stroke, and pass him. I never saw him again. I opened with an 11.06 first 100-meters. I felt good on the first inner turn. Crossed over on the backstretch, feeling low and connected to each stroke. I was feeling some lactic acid at this point in my legs. I set up the last outer turn. I was a little unsteady early but settled in for some good pressure. Exiting the turn, I was careful to stay with each stroke and not to look too far down the final 100-meters. After crossing the finish line, I looked up at the scoreboard; lap time was 28.93 and a final time of 39.99. This was the best start to a season for me, ever. Brandon set a personal best, which was good for him. I congratulated him on a fine effort. I suspect I gave him something to shoot for.

A couple of easy laps to start to flush the lactic acid from my legs. Warm-ups back on and a short rest before the 1000-meter race. The ice was being resurfaced, so coaches and officials got to take a little break. This was all a normal Saturday morning in Milwaukee.

About 40 minutes till my next race, so I went back on the stationary bike and did some stretching to keep warm and loose. When I returned to the ice, my coach at that time, Nancy Swider-Peltz Sr., stopped me to talk about the strategy for the 1000-meter race. I was in the seventh pair with Bill Armstrong, a fellow master. He would be in the outer lane, and I would start on the inner lane.

I opened with an 18.99 first 200-meters, cranked out a 29.90 for the next 400 meters, then hung on for a 31.40 final lap and a time of 1:20.29. Again, my best start to a season in the 1000-meter race, ever.

These times provided physical validation that I was on the right track with my decisions and priorities. I had set my goals and was clearly on my way to achieving them.

I am reminded of an analogy. I can equate myself to a piece of marble. When my piece of marble was created, I was crude and unformed. As I go through life, experiences chip away the marble to reveal my true self. My underlying beautiful sculpture is waiting to be formed by the elements of wind, rain, heat, cold, etc. A sculpture takes many thousands of blows by a hammer and chisel to form. The elements of nature also act on my raw material to change me.

The year 2012 was one of those years that changed me in many ways to help form my sculpture. I have been reminded quite a few times what is important. God, family, work, recreation, in that order. By sticking to those priorities, I can make decisions that are balanced. I cannot control the world around me, but I can change the way I react and respond to it.

I could list a number of events that have occurred during 2012 to illustrate my point. Suffice it to say that my wife's cancer diagnosis and successful treatment was at the forefront. The return of my 21-year-old daughter to my life was a blessing that I could not have foreseen but am eternally grateful for. Rescuing a puppy that ultimately rescued us. Work and skating issues were always present.

Life-changing events continued into that next year. I was the meet director and also a competitor for the third USA Masters International Single Distance Championships in Milwaukee, Wisconsin, on January 5th and 6th, 2013. I am part of an incredible masters movement. We had sixty competitors from four countries (United States, Canada, Romania, and Germany). The ages started at 30 and went to 80+ in 5-year groups. In fact, Vern Kappes (our 80-year-old) has been in continuous competition since 1939. His seventy-four consecutive year of racing speaks volumes about the sport of speed skating and about the masters athlete movement worldwide.

At that event, three masters world records were broken. We had numerous Mat 1 times reached, an accomplishment that makes skaters eligible for the honorary Masters National team and some state-of-the-art skin suits. Many skaters reached personal bests as well. We had a great banquet after racing on Saturday, followed by an open-forum discussion of many masters issues. Fellowship was continued at the home of the meet registrar Olu Sijuwade for a potluck dinner and to watch videos he made of the first day of racing.

This meet is always a great time to get together with my fellow masters competitors. I get to see old friends and make new ones. On Saturday, we raced the 500-meter #1 and the 500-meter #2 (the total time of both races determines the winner) and the 1500. On Sunday we raced the 1000, 3000, and the 5000-meters. At the end of the meet, we had an open 12-lap mass start race. (Everything else was time trials.) About 25 men and women put in $5 each. The pot was split between the first man and first woman racers. It was a very exciting race with some breakaways around the mid-point and with about three laps to go. The final sprint was the most exciting. The fastest man won by the length of a skate blade. We sure love to race, and our competitive side shows itself very prominently. In fact, the men's 5000-meter time trial race was won by .01 of a second.

I skated a 40.27 and a 40.22 in the 500-meter race, achieving third overall and first in my age group. The two men who beat me were in the 30-34 and 40-44 age groups. In the 1000-meter race, I skated 1:20.42—once again third overall (with the same two guys faster than me) and first in my group. I also skated a 3000, 5:06.53. I do not train for this event but treated it as a fun race. I was fourth fastest over all and first in my group. I am very proud of the fact that I was able to negative split the last four laps. I am a sprinter! Go figure.

All in all, it was a very successful meet for everyone. I was grateful to all who participated and to all who helped to put the meet on. I thanked my wife for her support and help as well. Also, I thanked my father Harold for coming in from Oklahoma for the weekend to support me.

The next weekend I went to Salt Lake City to race on the fastest ice on earth. My training and racing were progressing. I had a little time off from work and wanted to see what kind of validation I could find. I flew out on Wednesday evening from Chicago through Denver.

Skating Thursday afternoon, I was able to do some speed work. I was pleased with what I was able to accomplish because I clocked some fast laps, much faster than Milwaukee. The altitude is about 4,650 feet above sea level. Milwaukee is about 700 feet. About 80 percent of our drag is aerodynamic. With thinner air, you go faster. The ice was pretty fast too. The Utah oval was preparing for the upcoming World Sprint Championships the next weekend. Many world records have been achieved at this track. I've made the best times of my career there. I was able to adjust to the speed by setting up my turn entries earlier and choosing visual markers. I needed to get a feel for the pressure in the turns. My strength in my skating is my pressure into the ice through technique, not explosion. It requires a fine balance to achieve all-out max speed on the edge of a 1.1-millimeter blade and to stay in control. Falling at 35+ miles per hour is not something I like to do. I have a strong desire for self-preservation. On the other hand, I can push my muscles, heart and lungs to their limit.

Friday, I did a race warm-up with some extra work at top speed. After a good night's sleep, I mentally prepared for all contingencies. I felt ready to race Saturday morning.

Racing was delayed 15 minutes due to electronic timing issues. I tried to stay warmed up. First would be the 500-meter race. I started on the outer lane. I was off the line well. Got down low early and felt a pretty good connection to the ice. My pair on the inner was a runner, which is what we call a skater who has a very high leg turnover. I was taking three strokes to his five. He was ahead at the 100-meter mark by a couple of feet. I started my outer turn well and built pressure through out. Exiting behind my pair as expected (since he skated 15 meters shorter than me), I crossed over gradually and set up the next turn. I got my marks. I started the first crossover right on my mark. Then, I am not sure what happened. I slipped. In order to stay on my feet, I had to stand up and put both skates on the ice. My arms were not swinging as I tried to stay up. My legs were so busy trying not to fall that I don't remember if I took any more crossover strokes. As I exited the turn, I was able to get back down and resume skating. I was now even with my pair and got as low as I could and tried to make the most of each push for the final 100-meters. We finished almost side by side. My time was 40.63. His was 40.45. The distance between us was about the length of one skate blade.

At first, I was not pleased because I was expecting a much faster time. I was disappointed that I had slipped and had to salvage something. Gradually, I began to take a more positive view. It was hard to believe that, even though I had been unable to skate the second turn, my time was still a 40.

Even so, I had to analyze what happened during that bad turn. I put myself in this position. There is no one but me out there skating and racing. Training is one thing. Racing is another. I spend 99 percent of my time training, and I am very good at it. I also practice racing during training. Actual racing is different. When expectations and ego are involved, approaching the starting line is different. One thing that experience has taught me is that I still have to figure out a lot of stuff about myself and racing. That is one of the barriers I still have to conquer.

About 40 minutes later, I took to the line again for the 1000-meter race. This is my favorite race. It suits me best. I got a good start on the outer. I built nicely during the turn and really cranked the first long straight. I set up the next turn and really got good pressure. I came out of the turn even with my pair. I had the right of way since I was ahead by 15 meters and was going faster. I powered ahead to get clear and set up the next corner—the one that had been my nemesis 40 minutes before. This was the fastest I had gone all day, and I was now skating the same inner turn. This time it went well. I hesitated a little to make sure I got it right. Nice pressure, out of the turn, one lap to go.

Now I was feeling the lactate in my legs. Set up the next turn early and cranked it hard again. I drifted to the outer lane on the backstretch, crossed over, and set up the last outer turn. I have trained for this feeling; it was very familiar territory. Nice pressure and contact through the turn. Exit and stretch for the line. I knew I had skated a technically good race. I had given my all. My heartbeat, respiration, and legs told me that. This was a great feeling to have at that moment. So my time was a true reflection of what I am capable of producing. It was a season's best 1:18.85. I felt much better about the day's racing.

Next, I was back taking part in a typical weekend time trial racing in Milwaukee. About forty-five skaters attended to compete in races from 500 meters to 10,000. The ice was pretty fast that day, and a lot of activity was spread out among the two Olympic-sized hockey rinks, the 400-meter speed skating oval that surrounds the two rinks, and the running track outside the oval where many local athletes were running.

Leading up to that event, I had a very productive week of training and some good recovery. After I talked to my coach Nancy Swider-Peltz, Sr., we had a plan to do more high-speed work. I figured out right away what had happened on the high-speed second turn of the 500 the previous week in Salt Lake. My skate boot touched the ice in the turn causing the slip and near fall. To keep it from happening again, I made a skate adjustment between my left skate boot and blade. Building confidence, adjusting it twice more. That was key.

After a good warm-up off and on the ice, it was time to go. I had the first outer lane for the start. This is not my favorite lane because the second turn would be an inner lane and hard to hold at high-speed. However, I told myself I got this lane in the draw for a reason. I needed to work out my fears then and there; life was handing me another internal barrier to conquer. I was ready.

I approached the start with my usual mantra of gratitude, remembering that going all-out fast is fun stuff. Off the starting line a little late, but I got down quickly. Solid connection to the ice, every push working. Aggressive but patient. The first 100-meter opener was 10.72, my best ever. The first outer turn was also solid with good acceleration. Nathan Miller, in the opposite lane, was pretty close to me in the first 100, maybe a couple of feet behind. He beat me to the crossover, as we expected. Crossing over on the backstretch to the inner lane, I set up the next turn. I hit my mark, but after one crossover, I hesitated a little to feel the pressure. Then I started to crank it hard with confidence.

I shot by my competitor, who was in the outer lane now. Feeling pressure on my legs, never really conscious of skating, just feeling pressure into the ice. Because I have done so many turns in my life, I experience them as feelings instead of conscious action. I had 100 meters to go, trying to stretch for the finish line without losing any strokes along the way. Still putting good power to the ice. I skated past the electronic eye timer and looked up at the time on the scoreboard. 39.00! That was faster than I had ever gone in Milwaukee. It was a personal best for me at this rink. My previous best was 39.04, three years prior. I had just gone fast enough to qualify for the Olympic trials in December—where they would pick the next Olympic team for Sochi 2014. To qualify for this race distance in Milwaukee was extra special. My wife came to see me race that day and take some video. I was so grateful for her essential support.

I raised my arms in victory as I glided around the warm-up lane. I received many accolades from fellow skaters, coaches, and officials. They knew what I just did, and they showed their respect. I put my warm-ups back on and skated a couple of easy laps to start to flush the lactic acid from my legs. My feet were hardly touching the ice. I was floating, a job well done.

Forty minutes later, I was back on the ice for the 1000-meter race. This time I had the first inner lane, my favorite. I love this race—I love the speed, the technical demands, the conditioning required. My pair in this race was Brett Perry. He had just skated a 38.12 in the 500; he was going to be fast.

Good opener, nice pressure through the first two turns. This is what speed skating is all about for me. We go faster in this race than any other. The goal is to hang on to as much speed as possible without running out of gas too soon. This was a tough race. I beat Brett to the first crossover but not by much. He passed me on the third turn, on the inner lane. I tried to keep him in my sights. One lap to go, just trying to keep pressure, staying on my feet. Last crossover to the last inner turn. I saw Brett but could not catch him. He finished about 25 meters ahead. I looked up at the scoreboard, not knowing what to expect. 1:17.60. This was another personal best at Milwaukee. I still had some work to do to make the qualifying time (1:16.08). Then I started gliding in the warm-up lane. I had reached my goal for the season, but I could still add to that. I had the ability and now the confidence. I still had more racing to go at faster tracks. I was not done yet.

Goal achieved, barriers broken, 56 years of age and faster than ever! I am still good enough!

I realized that going faster was a choice, an intention. Getting slower was more about my conscious choices than my age or genetics. If I do the work, I get the results, independent of my age. When I understand the accountability for my choices, it frees me to achieve what I want.

CHAPTER WISDOM

Getting better and going faster is more about intention and choices than age.

PART THREE

PART THREE

CHAPTER 10

BUILDING NETWORKS FOR SUPPORT I: PARENTS AND GRANDPARENTS

When athletes ascend to the podium to receive medals, we rise on the shoulders of our support system. None of us can accomplish what we do without support. Parental support is the earliest and most foundational support most athletes receive. My brothers and I had the gift of compassionate, loving, and giving parents. At my brother Bart's gymnastics academy a few years ago, I observed a young girl who appeared to have talent. When I asked Bart about her, he said that she probably would not excel. He explained that she really did not have the parental support that was required to be successful.

His statement shocked me because our background was so different! During the 1950s and 1960s, our mother was able to stay home with us as we grew up. Our parents created an environment in which the expectation was that we could set out to achieve anything. They helped us figure out what we liked to do and how to feed those passions. Then they helped us set goals to get where we wanted to go—whether we were focusing on grades at school or sports. My parents' philosophy was that if we needed something to excel, then they would help us find a way to make it happen. That was our environment. So coming across something different was foreign to me. I finally started to see then how extraordinary our youth was.

Many people ask me if my parents were athletes. Yes, my father was the center on his high school football team at 5'6" and 150 pounds, and he also competed on the golf team, helping it to win a conference championship. My parents' graduating class had about fifty-five students in Webb City, Missouri, in 1949. My mother was a tomboy at heart, but she was not allowed to compete because sports were closed to girls back then. In later years, she became an accomplished bowler who competed at the national level.

My parents instilled in my two brothers and me the idea that we could do anything we believed. We took that to heart and are living proof. I am not extraordinary in my physique, height, strength, ability to process oxygen, etc. Although I am a middle-of-the-pack runner, I do have an ability that started with a thought, became a habit of thinking, and then created a belief that is exercised as faith in myself about what I can do. This sounds really idealistic, but I have proven it with tangible results. So I challenge you to do the same for your own lives.

My brothers and I dragged my parents to practice and competitions, not the other way around. The drive always came from us. There were many mornings at 6:00 am, driving to the Park Ridge Oakton Ice Arena to skate before school. We craved the activity, and they were happy to provide it. My parents loved to joke that the way to raise three boys born within five years of each other was to keep us tired. Sports was the outlet and focus we needed. We also grew up across the street from a park. We spent a great deal of time running, jumping, swinging, hanging from the monkey bars, playing ball, and skating there.

Another philosophy my parents had was that if we started a class or a seasonal sport, then we must finish it. No quitting in the middle. Yes, many times, I wanted to stop something halfway through. Flag football was one of those for me, but I stuck with it and ended up learning some lessons about myself that I would not have known if I had quit mid season. Specifically, I learned that I did not enjoy contact sports or running through crowds.

My brothers and I learned that we liked to set and achieve goals. The desire to go to practice had to be our choice, our commitment, our responsibility, and our reward. We learned this accountability, responsibility, and reward early. But parental support to set up this environment was crucial.

As an adult athlete, I still have parental support from my father.

He is a great cheerleader, confidant, and mentor. He still wants to contribute, so I encourage him to participate in any way he wants to. It gives us both great joy. My father is now over 83, and we have a closer relationship than ever. To this day, my father contributes financially to me by helping with coaching expenses, ice time, gas money, etc.

My mother died in April 2000. She remains with me in my heart and soul today. I feel her presence now and know that she is very proud. Both of my parents have had a profound influence in my life. When I came back to skating around 1997, my mother gave me $300 for new skates. I could afford my own skates, but she knew how much I loved the sport and she wanted to see me happy. Accepting her generous gift, I started skating again.

As a father myself, I want my kids to be happy and successful. My parents are the same way, and it is ok to let them still be my parents. I have also learned how to parent myself. After losing my mother to cancer, I needed to make that transition to learn to be my own advocate, to own my own power, and to build my own network of support.

Even though my mother is gone, I still feel her presence and influence. One philosophy my mother passed on to my brothers and me was to try all the sports and activities that we could until we found something that matched our spirit and physical capabilities. My brothers and I were all pretty good athletes. I tried a number of things before settling on speed skating. It suited me because I had great lower body strength, pretty fast running speed, and the stamina to do distance work. Since my younger brother Bart was only 21 months behind me in age, we were very competitive. Bart had great upper body strength and was exceptional at being upside down, so gymnastics suited him. Mike, my youngest brother, was five years younger than me and had the attitude of a scrapper. Because of that quality, he turned out to be a great short track speed skater.

Before I started concentrating on speed skating, I tried other things like swimming and soccer. When riding my bike, I was interested in how far, how fast, and what my limits were in speed and endurance. I was discovering patterns in my abilities as well as my psychological makeup. What was appealing to me? What fed me physically, mentally, emotionally, spiritually? Those were important questions to answer.

We always had to have some extracurricular activity. Just going to school and hanging out at the park was not OK. We needed to be challenged to do more than just schoolwork. My parents had their own support network too. They volunteered at our church to be adult supervisors of a teen group, as well as being active with other supportive parents.

When it came to physical support, I remember that our mother would provide all our meals. Sometimes I had to eat five meals a day to keep up with my caloric burn. My brothers and I sometimes had to eat at odd times of the day, depending on our practice and training times.

When I was about 13 and my brother Mike was 8, our mother would wake us up at 5:30 am, two days a week to skate. Short track ice was hard to schedule because it competed for ice time with hockey teams. The only time our Park Ridge Speed Skating Club could get ice was at 6:00-7:00 am Tuesday and Thursdays. I remember catching the bus to junior high school at 8:00 am. My classmates were still sleepy eyed. In contrast, I had already been up since 5:30, eaten breakfast, gone to the rink, skated an hour practice, gone back home, changed, and walked to the bus stop. My mother was there for us every step of the way, not a hint of regret, just undying support. That was her job, and she did it with a smile on her face every day. What my mother was doing then helped us to be the people we are today.

One weekend our family had competitions all over the state of Illinois. Mike and I had a short track event in East St. Louis. We went with another skating family in our club. Bart had a gymnastics meet in Champaign; our father accompanied him. My mother had an Illinois state championship bowling tournament in Peoria. After the competitions were over, we met in Champaign Sunday evening to drive home together. After that weekend, my mother decided to put aside her competitive bowling for a few years. She did resume it when it was not so much of a conflict and she could devote some time to practice again.

I have immense respect for and gratitude to my parents. Their commitment to support my brothers and me was our norm. I know now that was not normal for everyone, so I appreciate it more today than ever. Our parents provided the financial means to do what we did, paid the fees for racing, made sure we registered for the competitions on time, and volunteered for leadership roles in the speed skating club.

When I was older and able to work, my parents expected me to contribute financially so that I had a stake in my results. When I traveled to Holland in 1975 to train for the upcoming Olympic trials, I paid half the cost out of what I earned on my summer job. Flipping burgers at a golf course restaurant had more meaning when it helped fund my trip to Holland. Financial support for our goals was full when we were young, then tapered off as we got older. Having a stake in the financial aspect of being an athlete was important to teach us responsibility.

A recent conversation I had with my father demonstrated how my parents supported me in ways I never knew. I made the speed skating team to go to Europe after the Olympic trials but there was not enough money in the budget of the organization to send me. The officials of what is now U.S. Speed Skating approached my father after the 1975 Olympic trials with a proposal. They told my father that for me to go with the team to Europe, my parents would have to pay my way and it would be $20,000. In 2014 dollars, that would be more than $87,000. My father was taken back initially. Then he asked an important question: If I went to Europe with the team, would I be guaranteed a race in the Olympic Games? The reply was, "No guarantee."

My father did some quick calculations about how to raise the money quickly, but overall, he had a bad feeling about the whole thing. He never asked me what my opinion was about it; he kept it to himself. I am not sure if he even shared it with my mother. He saw how overtrained I was. He told me that he went back to the official who approached him and told him no. My father told me that it took a couple of years for him to figure out what had really happened. Essentially, the speed skating officials were shaking down my family for money. They saw a likely target and went after it.

I do not regret my father's decision. If he had done anything differently, then I would not be where I am today as a 747 captain at United. If he had figured out a way to send me to Europe with the team, I would have continued to skate. I would have probably competed for another Olympic cycle and put off school longer. By putting off school, I probably would not have the seniority I have at United today. I would have achieved more in skating as a youngster but maybe not return as a great masters competitor. Therefore, I am truly grateful for what my father did.

My father provided the leadership for me and our family in those formative years. He made the best decision, and I am proud that he went with his gut feeling. It has all turned out for the best. There are many rules in place so that kind of thing will never happen today. I am amazed that my father carried that burden for so long, and I have since expressed my admiration for his guidance and support.

My parents also felt that they should be parents, not coaches. We had seen too many instances where the parents were over-involved in the coaching aspect of sports with their own children. When the ego of the parent gets involved, decisions become cloudy, and the long-term welfare of the child gets sacrificed. Parents are the only people that can look at the long-term development of the child apart from the sport. The conflicting motivations are very complicated. The roles of parents and coaches are so different that to combine them is almost impossible.

My father was also great at behind-the-scenes actions. When Bart and I were in our early years of high school, he wrote to the NCAA to get the rule book about recruiting. When Bart was having a talk with a college coach, the coach suggested going out to dinner. My father told him that would be a violation of NCAA rules. The coach realized his mistake and said he should have known better since he was on the rules committee. I am grateful that my father did his homework to help protect us.

My grandparents were role models to me as well as my parents, and the lessons I learned from my grandparents are still with me today. I have a grandfather clock built by my grandfather Harry Hulsey, my mother's father. Pretty cool, huh? It is about 7 feet tall. My grandfather made this clock himself out of a walnut tree he cut down. He had the tree cut up and planed, then he dried it naturally in his barn loft for about 30 years. He was a carpenter by trade and after retiring as a maintenance manager of a chemical company, he wanted to get back to woodworking. He made a number of clocks before he passed away. I helped him finish his first clock. After my grandmother died, this clock was passed onto me. It stands in the corner of my living room today. When it chimes every 15 minutes as well as on the hour, it reminds me of him. When I raise the weights, it will run for 8 days.

One of the most important lessons I learned was from observing my grandfather winding his clock after church every Sunday. It seemed to me that he recharged himself on Sunday in church, and then he came home and wound the clock for the week. He was very involved with his church where he volunteered as a deacon and helped out with projects. The church was the main source of my grandparents' social life as well. During our summer visits, my brothers and I would get dressed up and attend church with our grandparents. I learned a lot from the way they approached their faith. I have my own way of recharging my spiritual batteries just as my grandfather did. On Sunday mornings, I wind the clock too. I remember how he lived and what an upstanding, respected man he was. As I try to live with him in mind, winding the clock helps connect me to his memory.

My grandfather bought a used 1969 Mustang for my mother to drive. That was around 1972. When I turned 16, I was allowed to drive that car to Milwaukee in the winter to train. This allowed my parents to support my younger brothers a little more. Years later, I realized that my grandfather really bought that car for me. Maintaining the car by doing my own brakes every summer, as well as rebuilding the carburetor every 6 months or so became a habit. One summer I drove it to my grandparents' house in Missouri, and my grandfather and I rebuilt the motor, power steering, suspension, brakes, tires, etc. I drove that car long after my skating career was over and sold it when it was totally rusted out. I gained some very valuable lessons about how to maintain an automobile from my grandfather. Those lessons serve me well today. It is probably one of the primary reasons I operate machines for a living.

CHAPTER WISDOM

The support of parents and grandparents comes in many forms and can be used throughout our lives.

PART THREE

CHAPTER 11

BUILDING NETWORKS FOR SUPPORT II: CHILDHOOD AND ADOLESCENCE

Gary Morava was a world-class collegiate gymnast and a friend to my brother Bart. He was a couple of years older than Bart. While on a trip with the U.S. team in Russia in about 1972, he saw people skating on roller skates with four wheels down the middle of the skate. We now refer to them as inline skates. Gary knew I skated and thought that these people skating in Red Square, enhancing their hockey skating skills in the summer, was revolutionary. He promptly bought a couple of sets of inline rollers and brought them home to me. I bolted some speed skating boots to them, and off I went. They were crude, but I could skate on them during the summer. They were much heavier than normal speed skates, but at least I could skate. The speeds were a little slower and I needed a pretty smooth surface, so a tennis court worked pretty well. Here was a great example of a network helping me when I least expected it.

In Morton Grove, Illinois, the northwest Chicago suburb where I grew up, we lived across the street from a park. In the winter, the park district would flood an area that had been slightly hollowed out to make an ice rink. They would put down new ice by using a fire hose every couple of days in the winter when it was cold enough. They would plow it to keep the snow off so we could skate on clear ice. There was a warming house that we could go into and warm our noses, finger, and toes. My brothers and I could also go home across the street, drink hot chocolate, and look out the picture windows of our living room 40 yards away to see what was going on at the ice.

My mother could keep an eye on us from this warm vantage point. She could see me racing from one end to the other as fast as I could go on my figure skates. She could see me playing tag and avoiding being tagged. She could see my brother Bart running on his skates as fast as he could and doing a front flip into the snow bank at the end of the rink. My brother Mike liked to speed around the rink with me too.

Dick Flickinger, who lived two doors away from us, was the mayor of Morton Grove. He came across the street to see me go fast. He had raced on speed skates as a teenager growing up in Chicago. Back then, athletes could earn a sports letter in high school for speed skating. He was impressed with my speed, so he suggested that I try something he loved, speed skating. He talked to my parents. They agreed to take a look at speed skating. After racing in a novice race in Park Ridge on my figure skates, I realized I was pretty competitive because I did well even though I raced against other boys my age who had speed skates. I decided to give the sport a try. You never know where you may be led in life. I am very grateful that Dick Flickinger saw me and wanted to pass on his love for speed skating to me.

A number of exceptional athletes lived in the local area where I grew up. The Chalapaty sisters, Celeste and Denise, were very competitive speed skaters. They both won numerous championships in the United States and North America. We shared many rides to the rink in Milwaukee to train. Bart and I were also among this group of athletes. Earl Numrich, a local businessman who wanted to help us financially, started a support group called the Niles Township Olympic Committee. This support group would raise money for local aspiring athletes. They would help to fund the gaps between the families and college support.

When I was about fourteen, I started working for a bike shop in Chicago after school and on weekends to make some money. Sometimes I would get a ride from my parents, sometimes I would ride my bike 45 minutes to get there. I helped customers with their bike needs, made sales, and sometimes assembled the bikes after pulling them out of the factory boxes. I also learned the value of a dollar, time, good customer service, and communication.

PART THREE

Growing up as a Boy Scout, I learned the Scout motto, slogan, and oath, and I carry those morals with me today. I started out as a Cub Scout, continued as a Boy Scout, and stayed with the organization into high school as an Explorer Scout. Through practical application, the scout program taught me many of the moral values I hold today. I learned how to be part of a group and work toward a higher goal, and I was able to see leadership in action and follow the examples to learn to be a leader myself. Scouting principles—striving for excellence, building my own integrity—are the qualities I strive for every day.

I was also able to provide a network of support to my brother Bart. One important incident occurred on a day when Bart was going to have an important competition in the evening. Because of the upcoming event, our parents had told my brother Mike and me to be nice to Bart that day. Bart and I were in high school at the time and had been out running some errands. We were bound for home in our shared 1948 Willys Jeep. Bart was driving. An older lady stopped her car suddenly in front of us on a busy road just short of some railroad tracks. There was no train approaching, no crossing gates down, no flashing lights, so it was a mystery why she stopped so abruptly. Bart tried to stop as quickly as he could but tapped her rear bumper. There was no damage to the Jeep, but there could have been a minor scratch on the already scratched bumper on her car.

Immediately, I decided that it was my job as the older brother to take over so that I could take the heat instead of Bart. Going through an emotional event a few hours before a competition would distract him, so I told Bart to move over and switch seats. We both got out of the car from our respective sides to survey what had happened. The lady got out of her car to come back to look. She was pretty upset. She told me that she was going to call the police. By talking to the lady, I calmed her down and handled the situation while Bart got back into the jeep. It took only a couple of minutes to look at the situation and realize that there was no real damage and that we could go our separate ways. The situation was diffused.

We got back in the Jeep and drove the remaining couple of miles home. It felt good to have resolved the situation with no lingering effects. In a few minutes, we were laughing at the whole incident, and by the evening's competition, it was a distant memory.

I recently learned, decades after the fact, that this situation and the way I acted had a profound impact on the way my father perceived me. He was more proud of me after this event than anything else I had done until then. Even though I felt great about what I did to help my brother, I had no idea that it would affect my father and his perception of me.

Here is another example of a chance meeting growing out of my network and leading to a greater network. During the winter of 1972-3, I was skating at the Olympic Oval in West Allis, Wisconsin, one evening. After I finished skating, I was in the warming house getting ready to make the 75-mile drive home. At the time, I was a junior at Niles West High School in Skokie, Illinois. Diane Holum, 1972 Olympic speed skating champion, approached me. She had been helping me as a coach during the previous summer with a training program. Because she lived and coached in Madison, Wisconsin, I used her mostly as an additional consultant while I was coaching myself. She had a favor to ask of me. A friend of hers, Steve (Grietus) Hilbrands, was visiting the United States from the Netherlands.

Steve was a fan of Diane's and had followed her career. He had been touring the United States after working in Canada during the summer. He was a college student in Groningen, Holland, studying clinical psychology. He needed a ride to Chicago to meet up with someone who was driving to Los Angeles. Diane knew I was going towards Chicago and wondered if I might give him a ride.

I had seen Steve around the rink and, since Diane asked me for this favor, I knew I could trust him. She introduced us, and we got in my car and started south towards Chicago and my home. We talked about our mutual connection, Diane. Steve told me what his plans were. As we talked on the drive, we hit it off pretty well. He was a skater, as was his younger brother Jacob. They both lived in an apartment in Groningen where they attended college. Steve was a pretty good skater and had followed Diane around Holland watching her race and cheering her on.

At that time, the United States had only a few artificially refrigerated, 400-meter outdoor tracks. In Holland, speed skating is practically the national sport. During the time Steve and I drove from West Allis to Chicago, we could have driven across Holland and passed nine rinks. The Dutch opened their rinks (outdoors were the only rinks that existed then) on the 15th of October, regardless of the weather. They had a rink in the town of Groningen too.

During the trip, I decided to stop by my house for dinner and to introduce Steve to my parents. Then I would take him to downtown Chicago, another 30-minute drive, so that he could meet up for his connection to Los Angeles. My parents were a little surprised at the unexpected guest, but they made a place at the dinner table for him. We all talked about sports, travel, etc. From time to time, we have had gymnasts from all over the world stay with us, so hosting a Dutch speed skater for dinner was nothing out of the ordinary.

This turned out to be a chance meeting that would have very significant implications. By the time I dropped Steve off in downtown Chicago, we had exchanged addresses and promised to keep in touch. We wrote back and forth a few times over the next year. In one of his letters, he offered me a room in his apartment if I wanted to visit or train in Holland. I wrote back and asked if the offer was real. He said yes. Since it was coming up on an Olympic year, an invitation to go to Holland to train on a rink that would definitely open on October 15th was priceless.

Steve and I continued to correspond by mail. I continued to train and skate hard. My plan was to go to Holland in the middle of September 1975 and be there for one month before the ice was available.

By saving the money I earned working during the summer, I was able to split the costs with my parents to go to Holland. I needed an airplane ticket, new skates, and food for the stay. Steve would provide a room in their college apartment as long as I chipped in money for food occasionally.

I flew nonstop from Chicago to Amsterdam on a KLM Boeing 747. I was a private pilot at this time and working on my commercial and instrument license at a small technical college in Kenosha, Wisconsin. About halfway to Amsterdam, I asked the flight attendant if I could go up to the cockpit to talk to the pilots. Back then, people could still do that. I told her I was a pilot working on my commercial certificate and would love to see the cockpit. I spent a half an hour in the cockpit with my eyes about as big around as dinner plates. The captain told me there was no co-pilot on the flight, just two captains. The captain was being given a check-ride by an instructor captain, who had taken the place of the regular co-pilot. The flight engineer showed me around his complex panel of fuel, electrical, pressurization, hydraulics, etc. We watched Venus rising from the east just before the sunrise as we flew over the dark north Atlantic. I wondered if this dramatic sight was a precursor for my future.

Steve and his father picked me up at the Schiphol Airport in Amsterdam. They drove me to Steve's parents house in Zutphen to meet the rest of their family. The next day we drove about an hour and half to Groningen. Steve moved his bed into the living room so I could have his bedroom for my stay. They lent me a bike to get around town easily. Everybody had a bike and great legs in that town. I learned my way around pretty quickly. When I began training with the local speed skaters off ice, they expressed shock that a U.S. skater would come to their little college town to skate and train. The better skaters would be going to the more well-known rinks, not Groningen. However, it turned out to be a good choice for me. Because Groningen was a college town, almost everyone spoke English. I did learn some Dutch phrases and could almost read the newspapers. Speaking Dutch was difficult, but I gave it my best shot. All the skaters wanted to speak English so they could try out their skills. They were much more adept at English than I was at Dutch.

When it came time to make the ice, I was there, actually helping lay down the first layers. In Holland with its moderate climate, they opened the ice rink October 15th, regardless of the weather. By being there, I was able to train and race well ahead of skaters who did not travel to Europe. My original plan was to return to the United States on November 15th, but I called home around the 10th of November and learned that they had no ice in West Allis because of a spell of warm weather.

When I asked my hosts if it was ok to stay a little longer, they said yes. I stayed a couple of weeks more to be assured that I would have ice when I went back and would not miss any training time. I have always been grateful to my hosts Steve, Jacob, and their family for their support at that time.

It might seem funny how a chance meeting led to this trip and opportunity of a lifetime. Was it chance or did my network set up the possibility for this to happen? I know the answer to this question. That is why I will always continue to develop networks. You never know what they can produce and how high you can fly.

CHAPTER WISDOM

Our networks are wider than we know and can work in better ways than we can predict.

CHAPTER 12

BUILDING NETWORKS FOR SUPPORT III: ADULT

For an adult, the support of a spouse can be very important. Trying to balance the responsibilities of a spouse or partner while training at an elite level for a sport can place difficult demands on any relationship. Maintaining and balancing priorities can be very tough. Sometimes my ego can get in the way and my priorities shift, and I don't even know it.

Spouses find it easier to support you if they have something at stake in your success too. If it is a shared sport, that is a plus. My wife Maripat is my biggest cheerleader. I spend a lot of time in the car between my home in Kildeer, Illinois, and the skating rink 75 miles north in Milwaukee. I am fortunate that the love of my life, Maripat, loves to come with me. We enjoy sharing our time in the car. Most of the time at the rink, she works out by riding a stationary bike or walking when I am on the ice. She loves to hang out with the other athletes whom we have adopted as our "kids." This is another chosen family for us, and we enjoy the experience together.

We did a nutritional analysis in the summer of 2008, which was more a test of how Maripat was feeding me than anything else. The analysis was done with all the data about my workload, body composition, etc. Even though the period we studied included a three-day trip to Frankfurt, Germany, and airline food, the analysis revealed that I was consuming exactly what I needed. Maripat does a better job with my nutrition than I am capable of doing myself by far. Sharing goals, balancing priorities, and spending time together create that essential support from my spouse.

Dealing with my emotions can be tough for me. I was afraid of my emotions for the longest time and felt it necessary to keep them at bay. Doing so is essential in my job as an airline captain. When I do need to connect with and express emotions, Maripat provides invaluable support. She helps me see myself. She provides a mirror so I can see where I am, good or bad. Maripat helps me a great deal by giving support during my emotionally bad times and helping me celebrate the good times. She can also help me set goals, so that we have a shared commitment. Whenever course corrections are necessary, then she helps me recognize the circumstances, shares my vision, and generates ideas to get to my goal.

I am reminded of the movie *The Rookie*. This movie was on television the other day and I had to sit down to watch it. It has so many important messages. One of the most important was when the dad, a rookie professional baseball player, was going to call it quits and come home. His wife asked him to consider what his young son would think and what the boy would take away from his action. The dad then reconsidered his decision and decided to stay with the farm team longer to see where he could go. He wanted to show his son what was important to him. Perseverance, dedication, courage, discipline, goal setting, and follow-through were some of the qualities that he demonstrated to his son.

Similarly, my kids learn way more from what I do than what I say. Just walking around a store can be a very educational experience. They learn how I deal with people, set goals, make choices, spend money, remain accountable, etc. The list goes on and on.

How I conduct myself during training and competition will teach my kids how to do the same thing, as well as help them apply such values to their lives. I am the example of a father they know best. They will likely repeat what I do as parents at first until they find their own way. How I conduct myself as an athlete; how I compete; how disciplined and dedicated I am; how I deal with disappointment, unexpected situations, and stress—all these will influence their approach to the world. My children have learned from my example.

It is also important to have my children on the same track. It would be great to be interested in the same sports. That way there would be some commonality, the same language, maybe the use of the same resources, time, etc. You may have to wait to pursue your sport as a parent-athlete until your kids are in school full time. You may have to wait until they are more self-sufficient, etc. That does not mean you have to give up your life for your kids, only maintain what you have until the time comes when your priorities can be more aligned. Having my kids support me as I have supported them can be priceless.

My parents told me that I did better in school during the time I was competing than at other times of the year. There are a number reasons for this. During periods of hard training and competition, many new neural connections were being made in my brain. As a result, I learned better and more effectively. When I am focused, my awareness is better. When time constraints become an issue, I become more productive with my time management. Training can take a great deal of time. As a result, I had less time for some of my other activities. The situation forced me to be more productive with my time, working smarter and better.

The same thing is true of me as an adult. I have found that I am a better employee while training and competing—healthier, more focused, and more productive at work. Even so, by getting my employer involved can help in a number of ways. For example, scheduling and arranging time off for competitions will be easier if they are already in the know. Cooperation rather than confrontation is the goal. Recently, I asked my employer for some time off for my fourth Olympic Trials. Needing time off over Christmas was a hard thing to ask for because it is such a busy travel season. My strategy was to approach my employers with the idea that this national exposure was going to be good for my company and my profession as an airline captain. Like all the other employees at United, I do many things besides fly airplanes and I am more than just my job. My skating is a prime example of something that I do outside of my workplace that has a direct impact on me as an employee. I am a better employee as a result.

I have a number of tools available to me through my employer. Access to those resources is essential, so allowing my employer to share in the rewards is also essential. Recognition for my accomplishments can be a boost to my ego, provide inspiration to others, and be good for the public relations of the company and my profession.

Having other coaches and experts in the field be a part of your network is also important. Giving respect and asking questions builds trust with other coaches. For example, my brother Bart's high school coach John Burkel would occasionally call in a coach from another area to help with a particular issue. This gave the other coach some respect and credibility. Then, if an issue occurred at a competition down the road, Bart and his coach John had an instant ally in any confrontation because the other coach had a stake in my brother's future.

John Burkel used this strategy because Bart competed in a judged sport in which decisions are subjective. You might be thinking that because my sport is purely based upon time, this consideration would not be a factor. However, any time human beings are involved in a competition, some judgment comes into play. In a sticky situation where decisions are made that might affect the outcome of a competition, having more advocates for oneself is always good. Because I developed good relationships with other coaches, they gave advice freely to me. I would listen, thank them and then decide to take or leave the advice. Those coaches, in turn, then had a stake in my performance and could be my advocate if necessary. This provides a network so when I have an issue with my training or equipment, I have many resources to draw from.

The more information I have, the better choices I can make. I can also encourage my coach to draw from many other experts in many different fields to build a more complete training program. Sometimes we get strength workouts from an Olympic weight lifter in Poland, our nutrition analysis from an expert in Argentina, etc. My coach's job is to put this all together for me, to tailor it, and to adjust it to the constantly changing conditions as I grow, change, and make progress.

A few years ago, I experienced a vivid example of how having a wide support network could help me. In the spring of 2008, I realized that my custom-made carbon fiber skate boots were starting to break down. I had already qualified to skate the upcoming Olympic trials in the fall of 2009. I wanted to make a good showing and needed the best equipment to do so. However, my boots were about four or five years old and starting to break down.

I had had them repaired from time to time by Scott Van Horne, who made them for me originally, but they were not holding up well. The blades—which were from Viking, a company in Holland—had also seen better days. I wanted to start the year off right with some new equipment. I flew to Calgary where Scott could mold my feet to make new boots. I rented a car, drove to his house, got the molds done in about an hour, then drove back to the airport, and flew home, all in the same day. The benefits of being an airline employee certainly paid off that day.

Then I needed to order new blades from Holland. When I first got the new blades, they were attached to some stock Viking boots. On first inspection, I spotted some quality control issues, so I returned them for another set. I did not realize it at the time, but the replacement blades I received were custom blades. The mechanism that attaches to the blade tube was for a size 40 boot, a European size equivalent to about a U.S. size men's 8-1/2. The blades were for a size 41 boot and were longer than stock by about one-half inch.

Because this was an Olympic year, I did not want to change too many variables. Making a major blade change could be difficult, especially since I would be adjusting to new boots as well. What I needed was to have a new set of blades that were as close as possible to the custom blades I had just worn out. A long time friend of mine, Nancy Swider-Peltz, Sr., had a personal connection with the guys making the Viking blades. Because of that, I asked her to help me. She was thrilled to do so. Nancy, Jr. (her oldest child), a member of the 2010 Olympic Team, drew a picture that included dimensions for clarity and faxed it to the blade shop in the Netherlands. After a couple of phone calls for clarification, all was set and the blades were built. The blades arrived in a pretty short order, they were perfect, and I was skating on them right away. I am grateful for Nancy, her daughter, and their network that was made available to me.

One reason I am able to build such an extensive network is that I wish my fellow competitors and peers good luck. I want them to do their best. I do my best, and I believe that the outcome of a race is always as it should be. I can say that because I know the results of a race were probably decided months before, based upon workload volume, training techniques, talent, focus, and a host of other factors. The execution of a race on the spot is important, but being faster than someone who is not at their best is no victory. Since I am competing more against myself than anyone else, I sincerely encourage my fellow competitors to do well. This helps me gain support from my fellow competitors.

For any athlete, the support of peers can be very valuable in a number of ways. It is hard to quantify what that support can mean. When I am not conflicted, I am more relaxed and can perform more to my capabilities. If I want respect from my peers, then I must give them the respect they deserve. I also must earn whatever respect they give me.

In addition to a network of coaches and fellow athletes, over the years I have developed a network of doctors and health professionals to help me on my path. It includes a complement of traditional Western medicine professionals as well as some Eastern medicine influences. I have an internist who pulls all the traditional Western thoughts and resources together, an orthopedic surgeon who can tend to my bones and joints, a staff of physical therapists to help with ongoing problems in recovery from injuries, an acupuncturist, and a reike master. For emotional support, I also get together with a group of men on a regular basis to discuss common problems. They are only going to help me if I am rigorously honest with myself about what is going on.

I have a lot of peers in many different areas of my life and it is up to me to develop, foster, and utilize these networks for my benefit and the benefit of those around me. Likewise I also find it a great help to give back to my fellows. I have realized that my long-term mental health depends upon giving back to the network I am part of. Sharing my experience, strength, and hope with others has two great benefits to me. The first is that is strengthens my self-esteem and builds upon my foundation. The second is that invariably I tell someone else exactly what I need to hear for myself. In this way, I get emotionally and mentally healthier. And of course, I may help someone else along the way.

CHAPTER WISDOM

Spousal support is extremely helpful. Other support can come from almost anyone to whom I have spread good will.

PART THREE

CHAPTER 13

GOALS

"It is good to have an end to journey towards; but it is the journey that matters in the end." Ursula LeGuin

Never underestimate the importance of goal setting. Seemingly impossible dreams can be accomplished when people focus on goals they can control. Many goals remain unspoken, motivations just under the surface. It is important to get those goals out in the open.

There is some risk in that. By telling someone about my goals, even by admitting them to myself, then I become responsible and accountable for them. This exposure can be daunting for some people. In addition, some goals can be a stretch, so they create the risk of going outside one's comfort zone. That can be a scary place.

The important thing is to make a start towards achieving the goal. If, after a while, it seems to be unrealistic, then changing the goal becomes necessary. It is ok to change goals and directions. Sometimes life demands it. When outside forces demand that goals be changed, I interpret that to mean that life threw me a curve. I must then adapt or suffer the consequences. When I find myself resisting change, I know there is a lesson for me.

Once I have a goal, I try to enjoy the forward motion of my journey as well as the direction. Then I achieve my goal because I am focused in the right direction. If I have no target or direction, I will surely hit something—usually, the thing I least want. But if I have a goal, a direction, a target, then adjustments are much easier to make. Even if I decide that the original goal must change, then at least I have made progress in determining my eventual outcome and I am farther down the road.

It is also important to look at my goals, no one else's but mine. Other people's perceptions about my goals are not important. My goals are my creation. If they become a burden, I must look deeper to the motivation behind the goal. A goal that oppresses me could be coming from someone else. I need to focus on goals that leave me feeling recharged, rather than drained, vindicated, or relieved.

I take a number of steps to set up my goals. First, I must know what drives me. This is a process that we go through for our entire lives. Knowing that I am driven to do things is a start. What am I passionate about? What are my priorities, and how can I fulfill them? Using fear to get started is one thing, but it is seldom the best motivation. Joy and passion will keep me coming back to completion of a goal or a positive change for a lifetime.

By using such questions, I determined that I have a passion for skating and skating well. It requires a great deal of work, but I am willing to do it. I have a passion for flying and doing it well, and it shows there too. So when I set my goals, I find it important to keep focused on passion and joy, and see where they take me. With these principles in mind, I set short, medium, and long-term goals.

Because I know my priorities, my goals will coincide with my values. Setting a time frame is next. Short range is a few months. Medium range is a year or two, and long range is five years or more. The farther out the time frame is, the greater the chance that I might need to change the goals. Breaking down the short range into even shorter time frames such as weekly, daily, or even, moment by moment can be done too. Each goal must be specific, measurable and have a time frame.

My parents stressed that it was important to set goals through an event. I stay focused on a particular event, but I also have another goal beyond it to transition to right away. Having a continuous path forward prevents any down time emotionally after the achievement. It is also important to savor the achievement and celebrate the event. Taking time for rest and reflection after the achievement needs to happen so that course corrections can be made. Usually after we achieve a goal, our perspective changes in ways we cannot predict. This is the time to evaluate and set a new path with a new perspective.

By knowing what direction to go, we can see a path forward. Then we take the big long-range goal and break it down into smaller pieces. We can outline the long-range goals that might take years, then the medium-range goals that cover only one year or one competitive season. Then finally, we create short-term goals that can be accomplished in months or weeks. I can also set really short goals that last only one workout or weightlifting set. Breaking my tasks into manageable parts is the key to making forward progress.

Here is an example of my goal setting. The long-term goal for skating is to qualify for the next Olympic trials. The time standards are set by U.S. Speedskating. The time frame for achieving these is during the season prior to the Olympic trials. I need to be in a position to skate specified times in that particular season. These are specific, measurable, time-sensitive goals. To accomplish them, I need to set up a training program for that season to compete at the highest level to achieve those times. Then I need to execute the training plan on a monthly, weekly, and daily basis. This is a general outline of what I do. You can make the plan as specific as you need for your own goals.

One hazard to avoid is sticking to a goal regardless of circumstances. Sometimes, my ego can take over to the point that I become a slave to the goal. As a result, I've learned never to give my goals too much power.

Similarly, I am a list person. My list can keep me on track, as productive as possible. But when I become a slave to my list, I feel overwhelmed, angry, and resentful. Here is where balance and priorities are important, so that my goals do not drive me, instead of me driving toward my goals.

After I achieve a long- or medium-term goal, I find it important to recognize the milestone. This can be done in a number of ways. Many families have rituals about celebrating goal achievements, such as going out to dinner, having a party, etc. I remember very vividly what I did after I qualified for the Olympic trials in December of 2005 at age 49. First, I made some phone calls to share the achievement. Then I went into the bathroom, looked myself in the mirror, and proclaimed, "I am good enough!" That was a very important moment for me, and I frequently remember it. It is now part of a solid foundation of my own self-esteem. This was my personal victory lap.

Another important quality of goals is that they do not have to be linear. They can change because of alterations in the individual, the environment, or the circumstances. A sign of maturity is the ability to change with new conditions. As we grow and change, so do our values, priorities, and goals. What seemed to be very important to me a couple of years ago may not seem so important now. As time passes, I have new perspective. Goals evolve as I evolve.

This reminds me of a book I read about survival. When it comes to setting goals purely for survival, the same principles apply, but the time frame becomes considerably shortened. In life-threatening situations, when all seems lost, the people who survive are the ones who can set short-term goals, celebrate their achievements, and move forward one step at a time. Some people survive astronomical odds by continuing the journey, literally one step at a time. By applying this same principle to a non-survival setting, people can achieve similar results. Break the goal down to much smaller tasks and continue to build on them step by step.

Managing expectations and setting realistic goals are also important. When I have unrealistic goals, I set myself up for failure. By setting realistic goals, I increase my chances of success. My ego wants me to have high goals for a number of reasons, but I need to keep them in check.

I do not like to apply the word success to goals. When we call someone a success, that is a vague term with a different meaning for each person. There is no way to satisfy the loose definition. I much prefer the term successful. To me, this term implies that being successful is an improvement based more on the individual criteria than some arbitrary cultural definitions. Evaluating whether I am "successful" is

PART THREE

better and more consistent than calling myself a "success" because I am looking only at myself.

I must communicate my goals with others who are important to my success, review those goals from time to time, and adjust them as necessary. Another important part of setting and managing goals is that we must change our perspectives as we go. To give an example, I remember a story about how I needed to change my goals based on a rules change by U.S. Speedskating.

The Winter Olympic Games of 2010 were to be held in February in Vancouver, Canada. The trials to make those teams were to be held in the fall of 2009. The trials were going to be held in two parts. The first part was going to be in the middle of October in Milwaukee, Wisconsin. The second part was to be in Salt Lake City in late December.

The bulk of the team spots were to be determined in Milwaukee at the U.S. single-distance championships and the fall World Cup trials. Olympic spots for each country were determined by results of the fall world cup events. A country could gain or lose spots based on its race performances. This made the fall world cup trials extremely important. As a result, U.S. Speed skating changed the rules for the Olympic team selection so that qualifying for the fall world cup events would be the criteria used to pick a majority of the Olympic team. In the past several Olympic games, the U.S. Championships meet in late December was where all the spots were filled.

In the past, we had all trained for and tried to have our peak performance at the Olympic trials competition in December. The new rules definitely changed the landscape. Typically, the skating season starts in late spring with off-ice training that lasts through the summer. For the previous few years, the indoor ovals around the world had shut down in early April. The earliest I have heard of new ice is early July in Salt Lake. Where I train in Milwaukee, we typically don't have ice until early September.

To train off ice, then transition to the ice in September, and be able to peak and race to qualify in October is next to impossible. The deck is stacked against the skater based on simple physiology. So U.S.

Speed skating helped to fund the rinks to get ice earlier in the season. In Milwaukee, we were able to skate in the middle of August. They had also changed the rules to make it easier to qualify for the fall world cup trials. You could now skate a qualifying time in the previous season.

U.S. Speed Skating set qualifying times based on a percentage of the previous year's twenty best world cup times. As elite world athletes get faster, so do the qualifying times. That particular year, the times for all the races except the 500-meter shifted faster. In the 500-meter the time stayed at 39.00 seconds. In the 1000 meter, the time dropped from 1:18.0 to 1:16.08. In the 1500 meter, the time dropped from 2:01.00 to 1:57.96.

My goal, which was just to make the trials rather than the actual Olympic team, was realistic for me. I wanted only to be part of that elite group competing in the Olympic trials. So now, I was able to qualify during the previous season. That was a big help to me; that way, I could skate a qualifying time over a season rather than in just a couple of weeks. At the American Cup Finale in Salt Lake in March 2009, I skated some great times. Typically my best times are in the spring at the very end of my racing season. That March, I skated a 500 meter in 38.47. I also skated the second-fastest 1000-meter ever for me, a 1:15.96. Unfortunately, I unknowingly touched two small corner blocks going into the first turn and was disqualified. I know what I had in my legs and in my heart, but the time didn't count.

My coach and I did not realize the true gravity of the rules changes, however, for this next Olympic trials. During the last trials in December of 2005, if you qualified in the 500 you could skate both the 500 and the 1000. In 2009, however, you had to qualify for each distance separately. Fair enough. I thought I could try in the fall to skate a qualifying time in the 1000 before the final trials in December. Then we found out in September that the qualifying times must have been accomplished by early October, not December. I had been training hard all summer trying to peak at the December trials. There is a certain method to our training regarding volume and intensity that plans for a certain peak performance in the season. We were planning for December. I wanted to do my best at the final trials in Salt Lake just as I had in 2005. When we found out that in order for me to skate the 1000 in December, I needed a qualifying time by early October, I was floored. We quickly had to adjust our carefully laid plans. After taking an easy week of training to taper off a little, I flew to Salt Lake to try and qualify. I needed a 1:16.08 or better.

The odds were stacked against me. The basic physiology was not supporting me. My goal had been to set up to skate well in October, then peak in December. We had not done much speed work, had not started to taper for speed and peak performance. Tapering my volume of work on and off the ice helps me recover from long, hard training so I can be at peak performance and speed. You cannot turn the body off and on quickly. Resting for a week was a help, but after hard training for months, an athlete typically takes a taper of several weeks.

Despite the long odds, I gave it my best shot. Skating a one-day race warm up in Salt Lake, I was careful not to overexert. Then I skated only one race, the 1000. Typically I will race the 500 and then an hour or so later the 1000. I gave it my best shot and finished with a respectable 1:18.25. A little more than 2 seconds too slow. I returned to Milwaukee knowing that I would race only the 500 in October as well as December.

In the months leading up to this major event in Milwaukee, the rink was changing. Randy Dean, the director of the Pettit Center was transforming the building. New flooring had been laid in various spots around the building. The hockey boards and glass had been taken down on the inside of the oval. The crowd could see the racers all the way around the oval. The stands that were normally adjacent to each hockey rink were moved to the outside of the oval for better visibility. New banners advertising the event hung everywhere, inside and outside the building. Temporary tickets booths were set up outside the main doors for the public to get their tickets. The athletes and officials needed passes to get past the ticket takers as well as into the secure areas of the building. The ice was off limits to everyone except the athletes and coaches. The media had limited access to the athletes and had to stay behind barriers in the tunnel leading to the ice.

The 500, my only event, was going to be held on a rainy Wednesday evening. The competition would be the total of two races that evening. In the first race, I would start from the inner lane, then in the second race about 90 minutes later, I would start on the outer lane. The total of both times would determine the results.

I was paired with a young man I have raced with many times, Lee Eckert. He was a 20-year-old student at Marquette University, working on his degree for architecture. We were introduced to the crowd, and then we took to the starting line. Lee and I came off the line together and were step for step for about the first 40 meters. I was able to get a lead by the first 100-meter mark, then I entered the first turn. I never saw Lee again in this race. I came out of the first turn ahead and finished that way. It was a pretty solid race. I was still interested in peaking for December, but I wanted a good showing there.

That event in Milwaukee in October 2009 was a very special occasion for many reasons. I had a lot of people cheering me on from the stands: Maripat, my father Harold, my uncle Dee, my brothers Bart and Mike, my son Brad, and my friends Steve Heaviland, Hal Edwards, Vic and Sheri Pfamatter, and Chuck and Maureen Prettyman. This was a great support network. Most of the people who support me do not have the ability to see me compete in person. Having the first set of Olympic trials in October in Milwaukee made it possible for all my supporters to see me race.

After my first race, I was on cloud 9. I was making a good showing, right in line with my expectations. It was not my best time ever in Milwaukee, but it was that season's best time. The important part was that I was there competing at my age.

When the previous pair crossed the start line with 100 meters to go, Lee and I both glided out to our start lanes for our second race. We acknowledged each other and wished each other good luck. The announcer introduced us, and we were called to the line. I lowered down into position for the start, same as before, but this time I was on the outer lane. I beat Lee to the 100-meter mark again. He had the first inner lane, and we came out of the first turn with him in the lead by about 10 meters. The goal was to catch him on the backstretch. As I crossed over to the inner track, on the back stretch, my timing was a little off. I was trying to force the stroke. I felt myself losing control and twisting sideways. Once it started, I couldn't stop it. The next thing I knew, I was sliding on my back halfway down the backstretch. My race was over.

I slid through the entry for the second turn all the way to the pads on the outside of the track well behind Lee. Nothing was hurt, just a bruised ego. Crossing back over to my lane, I finished the race and received a nice round of applause from the crowd for finishing. Because I was behind Lee when I fell, I didn't cause an impediment, but I was disqualified because I slid through to cross the outer lane. Oh well. I had still achieved my goal of competing.

I put on my warm ups, turned in my armband, and skated a few easy laps to try and stay loose. From the warm-up lane, I watched the other men competing. After about 10 minutes of cool-down skating, I stopped, took off my skates, and packed up my skating bag. I walked back through the tunnel to Dave Cruikshank's workout facility. I got back on the stationary bike for 10 minutes and then I did a nice cool-down stretch. It was starting to sink in now what had happened. I was able to get out of the pinpoint focus and look at the wider view. All of the people in my support group were there at in the workout facility, sharing my success of competing at this level.

Several reporters wanted to speak to me after I skated. The New York Times reporter, Bart, my father, and I had a great interview. One of the questions stuck out for me: The reporter asked Bart how he felt about me competing at this level at this age. Bart said, "I am very envious. I feel a little jealous that he can still compete and fulfill his passion for his sport." Bart knows that, even though he is still active in gymnastics as a gymnastics academy owner and part-time coach, his competitive career has been over for some time. He can never repeat what he used to do because of age and injuries. In contrast, I am very privileged to be able to continue at this high level. Due to the nature of my sport, my longevity can be extended by doing the right things to stay healthy. I am willing to do the work and make the many decisions every day to keep training and competing at this level. It's not just for the sake of competing and performance. I do it because I love it, and it feeds me and enhances all the other parts of my life in immeasurable ways.

After the fall trials, I returned to training hard for the final Olympic trials to be held in Salt Lake just after Christmas. My main goal was to compete at a high level at the next set of trials. I was at the rink four to five times a week, doing twelve workouts per week, and flying as well. I was having some trouble getting the time off for the trials. With my seniority at United, I could not be guaranteed to get Christmas off. The 500-meter race would be on December 26th. In order for me to do well, I needed to be in Salt Lake a few days before. The ice is faster there than at the Milwaukee rink, and some time on the ice is necessary for a smooth transition and an opportunity for fast times. The chief pilot of United Airlines' Chicago base helped me to get some vacation days before Christmas so we could travel and prepare.

Maripat and I flew to Salt Lake on the 23rd. I was able to skate the afternoons of the 23rd, 24th, and 25th. This was not a normal Christmas. At the last trials, I flew out on the evening of Christmas day and raced on the 27th and 28th. This time was different. We had to go out earlier, and I was going to have only one race day. Spending Christmas racing, away from our families was hard. Maripat was with me but not my immediate family. I would not see my kids, my father, or my brothers and their families. Maripat would not get to see her two boys in Boulder or our two grandchildren. Sacrifice can be painful this way. We would have to make time to see all of them after the holidays. But we had our skating family with us. We are a like-minded group, and we all know the sacrifice it takes to achieve. I was trying to do something that no one else had done, trying to leave a legacy, leading the way in the only way I knew how. I would have more holidays, but I didn't know how many more races I would have. This was my time.

To the other skaters at these trials, this might be the most important time of their skating life. So few Olympians medal. To make it to an Olympic games can be a great addition to a resume. I was grateful to be a participant, gliding around the track with a feeling of gratitude and fulfillment that was hard to explain. Skating faster than ever in my life, suffering through a knee injury and surgery five months before. Newly divorced, I had grown in ways I could never have foreseen, and through it all, skating was my foundation. Here was a way to feed my soul. Here was a way to diffuse my anger. Here was a way to help define me. Here was a way to heal some very deep wounds from my first marriage and my childhood.

I had a sense of peace and belonging. I was at home with my fellow skaters on the rink. Maripat says that when I skate by, unless you see my face, I look just like all the other 25-year-olds. My physique is the result of how my body responds to the skating and training I do. I guess it fits that I look like everyone else on the ice because I do the same work.

I skated some very respectable times at the trials, which were actually faster than my times four years prior. As I finished with a sense of pride and the underlying "knowing" that I was where I belonged, I had a far-off sense that I would be back in four more years. It reminded me of a Ralph Waldo Emerson quotation: "The future belongs to those who prepare for it."

I was feeling good about the hard work I had done, just as a craftsman is proud of his creation. I had achieved the goals I set for skating. I was proud of the work just as a craftsman is proud of his creation. I accepted myself, my journey, and the healing it had provided for me. The deep-down satisfaction of the goals achieved provided me with the self-respect I was looking for. I have done a lot of work to find the roots of my driven nature. I want to be accepted, loved, appreciated, and admired. The recognition was more from myself, than anyone else. As my father wrote about me, "Maybe he strives for the goal of self respect."

When I got serious about skating in my teenage years, I set some lofty goals after some success at the national level and being named to the national team (the only benefit was being on the list). Realistic or not, I aspired to be on the Olympic team, to compete with the best, and who knows, to set some world records. In 1972, Dutch skater Ard

Schenk was the first man to break two minutes in the 1500-meter race. To me, that was amazing, and I wanted to accomplish something similar.

In March of 2009, I was completing a great season of training and racing. I went to Salt Lake to race in the season-final American Cup. During this competition, I skated my best ever 500 meters in 38.47 seconds. I skated this exact time twice on successive days from different starting lanes. I also had a great 1000-meter race at 1:15.96 (second best ever), but I was disqualified for touching a corner block. I knew what I had in my legs that season, and it was magical.

I have worked very hard at learning how to go fast. Although I don't have the explosive power that pure sprinters have in the 500-meter, I can get to top speed and keep it for longer than the pure sprinters. That is why I am so good at the 1000-meter. The 1500-meter, however, is the race of truth. It requires speed, technique, endurance, and energy management. You get to see what you are made of. At the end of the race, you are totally focused on staying on your feet, keeping speed with good technique. When you're exhausted, your muscles are screaming and tightening, your lungs gasping for air, your vision narrowing to a tunnel due to oxygen debt, all while you are staying on the 1.1-millimeter wide blades and finishing the race.

I am so proud of that 1500, proud because I kept it together and finished so well. Coming through the last turn, I maintained a good constant pressure and kept my tempo up as much as possible considering the tightness building up with my legs swollen from the lactic acid. Exiting the last turn onto the home straight, 100 meters to go, I was careful not to look up at the finish line. Focusing on each stroke, remembering my father's words in his poem about me on that frozen lake when I was young: "Each foot under body starts." I kept my technique intact and my speed to the finish. During the last ten strokes, I saw the reflection of myself and what I was made of: Strong, willing, having the guts to dig deeper than ever, and possessing the technical expertise, the equipment, and the support. Knowing that I did all that I could do, I was pleased. I crossed the finish line by myself; my pair in this race was not important. Racing myself and winning the goal of self-respect was what mattered.

I rose up after the finish line knowing that I had truly done my best. This was a deeper feeling than any other in my racing career. I had experienced a great deal as a masters skater. This was somehow different. I didn't even need to see the scoreboard; I knew in my heart it was good.

Eventually, I did look at the scoreboard for official verification. I had broken 2:00! I had worked hard, and here was the tangible result 1:59.41. Gliding along the backstretch, coasting into the warm-up lane, I was congratulated by the coaches and my peers for my accomplishment. This was an all-time personal best for me in the race of truth. My fastest time in 1975 as a 19-year-old was 2:16.0. This was a huge leap for me. Here, 34 years later, I was 16+ seconds faster. At the speeds that I travel in that race, 16 second equals one half lap faster, about 200 meters ahead of myself as a youth. The time and effort it took to accomplish this one task was staggering. It was worth every bit of it. I still carry this feeling of satisfaction with me to this day and always will. Looking back, I saw that breaking 2 minutes had been a hidden goal of mine. Now I had done it.

CHAPTER WISDOM

By enjoying the journey as well as the finish, I use goals as my vehicle for making external and internal progress toward wholeness.

CHAPTER 14

EGO AND EMOTION

I do not regret the past nor wish to shut the door on it. If things had been different back in my past, I would not be the man, father, husband, masters skater, and pilot that I am today. I have learned a lot of lessons from my past, and I continue to do so as long as I stay open and conscious to the messages that come my way. Only recently have I come to a deeper perspective about what happened in my youth, how I responded, and how it shaped my life. No regrets, just profound lessons on my path.

Do I attempt to compete with my brother Bart, the Olympic champion? Yes, there is probably some truth to that. Each of us needs to find out how and why we are motivated. By using this knowledge, I can make better decisions about who I really am, what pushes me around, and what drives me and my ego. After I know these truths about myself, I can see what works and what doesn't.

I have asked myself the question many times, "Why do I do what I do?" Being an introspective person, I like to look at the root causes of my behavior. I do not know that I will ever make sense of it all, but it is important for me to look at what my underlying motivations are. Even though I made many mistakes (that did not seem like mistakes at the time), I need to examine the root causes. It is important for me to figure out my thought process, how I went wrong, and how to make changes for the future. I do not want to repeat old mistakes. Learning from them without passing judgment on myself helps me to change my responses for the future.

If I were to live without looking at my past mistakes, I would be doomed to repeat them. To me, that is hell. To break this negative cycle, I must first know what my underlying motivations are. This takes a great deal of work. However, the rewards are amazing.

One of the things I have learned through self-analysis is that my ego plays a large role in driving me. Meditation—as well as talking to my spouse, relatives, trusted friends, and therapists—are some of the methods I use to get to my basic ego-driven thoughts. The most important element of the process is honesty. I must be as completely honest with myself as possible. I heard a phrase once that makes a great deal of sense where honesty is concerned. "Between you and me is just air, but between me and myself is a lifetime of denial." My honesty is a fluid thing. As I change and grow, my concepts change and so does my sensitivity to my own honesty. I am better able to tell now if I am being honest with myself than I was several years ago.

The whole purpose of this train of thought is to discern what my basic motivations are. Is my ego pushing for something that will impact the rest of my life in a bad way or in a good way? For example, I must examine my need to be successful at speed skating. Do I do this because I am competing for the love and attention of my parents as a child? If that were true, it would override everything else and all my decisions would be based with this in mind. I have grown beyond that simple concept now. As an adult, I can show you that I skate and compete for the pure joy of it.

My ego is ever present in my life. It rears its ugly head at times, but it is not all bad. Many times, it helps keep me motivated towards my goals. Going through the process to find out what influences my ego has yielded great insights to my own deep-down drives. The goal is always to work through these issues and come to a peaceful place where my ego is concerned.

My ego has many positive influences on my life. The important thing for me to remember is that I am in charge, not my ego. The ego is only one part of my existence. I can use it to my advantage, or it can drive me to destruction if I leave it unchecked. My ego and the need to achieve can keep me on track, focused, and driven, as long as I keep my priorities straight. If my ego takes over, then my goals can become a new priority. They come to overshadow everything else, what is really important to me, and I lose balance.

At the Pettit Center where I skate, a quote from the famous basketball coach John Wooden hangs on the wall: "Sports does not build character; it reveals it." I love this quote. In my own life, I have found that through trial and hardship, my true character is revealed. I am made up of raw materials. When a conflict happens or something causes me friction and heat, I respond by changing. Then I become more like who I was meant to be. Like an alchemist who takes raw materials and heats them to try to transform those materials into gold, the heat of conflict, change, and competition can help reveal who I really am.

I have found a few passions in my life. One of them is flying airplanes, another is skating. These activities feed my soul. I believe that if I am enthusiastic over the long term about something and I keep coming back and wanting more, then it must be feeding a deep need in me. It may take me years of introspection to determine what is going on. I find it helpful to ask myself, "What does this activity do for me? What do I like about it? What keeps me coming back? What keeps me exploring and wanting to go deeper?" These are very important questions.

It is hard to make snap judgments about what feeds my soul; I need to look at my behavior in the long term. If I am floundering around for a long time, maybe I have not yet found the thing that sustains me. A good honest appraisal will reveal a great deal. One sure sign that an activity feeds me is that I will miss it and long for it when I have not done it for a while.

Something that feeds my soul is very different from other things that I do. If I elect to do something out of love and gratitude, that is usually a sign that it is feeding my soul. In contrast, an addiction will take hold of me and control me. If I am engaged in something that is more like an animal need, without anything more than immediate gratification, it probably does not feed my soul and will not be beneficial to me in the long run.

As I look at the influence of ego in my life, I find a never-ending process at work. Ego is a powerful influence in my life, good and bad. The ego will always be present and it is up to me to decide how to treat it and how I allow it to influence me.

I can also embrace it for what it is, a self-fulfilling entity. My ego cares about nothing but itself and its satisfaction—but I can use it to my advantage. In the context of achievement, I can use my ego to help drive me and keep me focused. In the context of just being a human, then I must park the ego influence.

If I am constantly changing, then my ego is also constantly changing and adapting new ways to exert its influence. To my way of thinking, the ego is a short-term thinker looking for quick gratification, and it is never truly satisfied. As a higher being, owning my own power, I can create valid boundaries for the ego's negative influence and harness its great potential for the positive motivation and drive it can exert.

I can be motivated by a number of things besides ego—namely love, fear, and anger. After experiencing all these emotions in my life to different degrees, I have learned that it is up to us to choose how these emotions will affect us.

I don't mean to imply that we have control of our emotions; we do not. Feelings are just feelings. Feel them, then let them go. They are transitory. The physical chemical aspect of any human emotion lasts for only about 90 seconds. When we choose to let go, the feeling will pass.

If instead, we avoid emotions or refuse to feel them, we suppress them. Those suppressed emotions will manifest themselves in many ways, either in our behavior or our physical condition. For example, anger goes to my gut, issues around money go to my lower back. I am still discovering how this works and continually working at dealing with this aspect of my life.

Whether to face emotions sooner or later is a choice we all make. Later will always be harder. Early in my life, I did not know how to deal with my emotions, good or bad, and I repressed them. I would deal with them only if it was too painful not to. Being a sensitive guy, I don't like to get hurt, so I used to have a two-day lag when feeling strong emotions like fear and anger. That was my buffer. I would let myself feel the raw anger two days after the incident, thus minimizing the impact. I can appreciate my emotions much more now and allow them to add the essential color to my life. I'm even getting better about feeling love right away.

Fear is also a very powerful emotional motivator, and I have found it can serve some very useful purposes. Fear keeps me safe. Fear keeps me from speeding down the highway at 100 miles per hour. Not fear of being caught, but fear that I might get hurt or cause someone else to be hurt, cause damage, etc. Fear can be bad as well. If left unchecked, it can push me around in strange ways. Mostly, I struggle with fear of pain. I may go to great lengths to avoid pain and the underlying fear.

Anger keeps fear at bay; it puts space between me and the fear. It is a way to create a barrier that I can control. When the anger subsides, I can address the fear and emotional pain. Anger is an offensive move to keep the fear at bay so we can process it our own time. However, I've learned to be careful not to hold up the anger barrier too long because it will turn into resentment. Resentments poison me over time by causing me to continually re-feel the original anger and pain. Our brains do not know the difference between emotional pain in the past or present. Resentments eat their own containers, namely us. The poison of resentment eats us up over time, deals us mortal blows, and keeps us from being peaceful, happy and serene. Anger can also be turned inward and cause self-destructive behavior.

The best antidote for this way of thinking is self-acceptance. One of my characteristics is being self-critical, and when carried to an extreme, that quality can be a defect instead of an asset. I need to balance this with gratitude and acceptance. My self-critical and perfectionist nature can help me achieve great things. But at what cost? If I tear down my own self-esteem in the process of achieving a goal, what is the value in that?

Being happy with who I am now does not mean I stop trying to improve. I used to call myself a perfectionist. The ideal of perfection is not possible in any universe and there is no balance in that place. Although I always strive for excellence, I try to balance the relentless press of my spirit to do better, learn, and grow with the choice to be happy with where I am. Balancing my ego so that it is useful but does not control me.

I compete more against myself than anyone else, so I judge and compare my current self to my former self. This is my true competition. This approach works well because I compete in a sport that is measured impartially by time. Striving for progress is the important measure. Progress can be measured many ways and is not always linear. As long as a person has a goal, progress can be made. As goals can come in many forms, so progress can come in as many forms.

One aspect of understanding my ego is that I am not so special as my ego would have me believe. We are all unique. Even my brothers have a different perspective on life than I do. Even so, I have more similarities to my fellow humans than differences. My ego would have me be different from everyone else, to set me apart. Ego keeps me isolated. In contrast, feeling part of and connected to humanity is what is important. I take great comfort in being a part of groups that think like me and that help me understanding that I am not alone.

We all have different "tribes" that we belong to. We have a biological family, families we have married into, and chosen families like my skating group. These different families are part of a support network that I give my time and energy to. Tremendous energy and healing can come from the families that we belong to.

When considering my ego and how to deal with it, the people with whom I spend my time and the ways they deal with their egos are very important. I must choose whom I hang out with. For example, when I train with world and Olympic champion speed skaters, I take on their way of thinking. That gives me a better chance of seeing what works in my sport and of following their example. I will not achieve what they do, but when I believe that I can, I will do better at all aspects of my life. We become more like those around us just by exposure, then by practice. Therefore, by being around people who deal with their egos in healthy ways, I become better at doing so myself.

This is another reason I like to be around young people—it helps keep me young too. I learn a lot from young people, such as unbridled enthusiasm, new perspectives, etc. In turn, passing on my wisdom and knowledge to them strengthens my own concepts and values, especially with ego and emotion.

CHAPTER WISDOM

Recognize and deal with your ego and emotions to your advantage.

PART THREE

CHAPTER 15

THE "A" GAME

Discipline is the trained state of mind translated into consistent actions. Consistent actions result in movement towards my goals. I make many decisions every day that affect my health, goals, achievement, and performance. Reminding myself of my goals and direction will help me stay on track until the desired behavior becomes automatic. People can use many different ways of sticking with a goal and having the discipline to follow through. How important is the goal to you? If it is really important, you will find a way. How valuable is it to you? Make the commitment; you are worth it! Enjoy the journey towards your goals while smelling the roses and enjoying the process along the way.

When I think about racing, my heart rate immediately increases. As I visualize the approach to the starting line, I repeat my pre-race mantra to myself. When landing a 747, I am totally focused on the job at hand. I do not think about what to pick up at the grocery store later. These are important character traits that maybe I was born with or that maybe I have developed over the years. I can tell you that I have fine-tuned them to what they are today. I will never have it down perfectly, but I continually make progress. This takes practice.

When I'm in training, I bring my "A" game to everything. This means I give my full effort, on every level, even if it means going to total exhaustion. This takes some emotional energy. My emotional energy can be restored pretty quickly, faster than my body can recover. For example, when I'm doing a sprint workout, I simulate a start. Practicing a start from a standing position requires precision. I could just crouch down, explode off the start line, and complete the effort. Instead, I repeat the entire process as if I'm in a real race—including saying my mantra, stretching as I would before approaching the line, acknowledging my competitor, and imagining hearing the starter's commands and the gun shot. This allows me to experiment with my mental state during this process. Using emotional passion and energy each time I practice helps me to summon it up when I need it for a race. What works best for me at the start of a race is relaxed but focused, then when the race progresses and my energy is being drained, I summon my deep-down strength and force of will. What works best for you? Experiment with many approaches and find what works best with your personality. There is no right or wrong.

Practice with focus. I practice physical activities so that I can fine-tune the mental aspects of my training. I practice the mental thought processes so that I perform better physically. The physical and mental are mutually supportive.

My self-talk can be brutal. In order to for me build confidence, I must speak kindly to myself. Self-esteem is an inside job; I am the only one who can affect it. To have success, to accept myself as I am, I build my own self-esteem through positive self-talk. I do not like to be judged by others because I am harder on myself than anyone else can be. This mindset is self-defeating.

The attention I give to the task at hand must equal my intention to achieve the goal. If I am intent on accomplishing a goal, I must not go through the motions mindlessly but with purpose.

All growth must be allowed, not forced. It must happen in its own time and way. If I force growth, I shortchange myself, and I must repeat the lesson until it is learned correctly. The universe will help me to repeat something until I get it right. I become what I believe. You cannot turn a cruise ship on a dime. It takes time to change the inertia. Similarly, it takes time for me to change my mind and concepts.

It is well known that it takes about 10,000 hours of any activity to be an expert. Building the neural network for consistency and expertise takes a great deal of repetition with focus. Once the nervous system has repeated an action correctly enough times, the connection is solid. Then it takes much more repetition to build the myelin coating over the neural connections in the brain and to the muscles to assure that the connection will stay strong through all conditions. When training as a speed skater, I build my motor for propulsion (muscles) and the brain and nervous system connection to apply my motor to the ice.

Making the commitment to this process is up to me and only me. A friend recently asked me to recommend the best exercise to do. My response was anything a person can do everyday is the best. If you go to the gym and do something you do not particularly like, then chances are you will find a way to stop. If it does not feed your soul, then it probably drains it. You can only drain for so long, and then you will find a way to stop. It may be through de-motivation, a shift in priorities, an injury, etc.

I will not spend time doing something that will not benefit me in some way, even play. You have probably heard the expression no pain, no gain. You must push to break down your muscles so that when they rebuild, they will be stronger. However, to push in a direction that is fundamentally wrong will only result in being tired, angry, resentful, and soul-depleted. Our bodies talk to us, providing physical symptoms to recognize so we can make course corrections. When I am aware of what my body and my gut are telling me, in tune, in the moment, then I have a chance of making good decisions. I cannot change what is outside of me until I change what is inside.

I must accept my circumstances that are both outside and inside of me without judgment. That does not mean I have to like them to accept them. It means refraining from wasting my energy trying to change things I cannot change and making a new decision as a result of acceptance. To move forward, I must accept people, places, and things just as they are—and myself, as I am.

We are constantly changing and moving, never static. It is easier to accept myself knowing that I am not static and that I can and do change all the time. It is my purpose in this life to live, learn, and grow till the day I die.

One of the jobs I had in my flying career was for a small commuter airline in Fayetteville, Arkansas. The airline was called Scheduled Skyways.

My primary job was as a commuter captain for Scheduled Skyways. The company also owned a fixed-based operation that sold fuel, an airplane charter business, and a flight school. I trained the pilots in the charter operation to fly the Cessna 310, a light twin that seated six people including the pilot. As chief flight instructor of the flight school, I oversaw about five part-time and full-time flight instructors.

One of my multiengine students was also one of our flight instructors. I sent him to a local FAA designated examiner to get his multiengine certificate. He passed the check ride, but what he told me about his certification flight made me ask a few questions. I called the office in Little Rock where the local FAA office was and shared my concerns with one of the inspectors there. This particular inspector had ridden with me a couple of months earlier on one of my regular line trips on the airline, and he liked the way I ran my operation as a commuter captain flying 19-seat turboprops. The examiner who had given my student the multi-engine check-ride retired, and the FAA inspector asked me if I wanted the job. I said yes! It would look great on a resume.

I went to Oklahoma City for a week of training, then some local training with the Little Rock office, and then certification checks for private, commercial, instrument, and multi-engine. The minimum age requirement was 23. I believe that I was the youngest ever to get the job. All the other trainees in Oklahoma City were at least 20 years older than me. I felt so honored to be treated as an expert in my field. Funny how things turn out. Because I pushed forward, always doing my best, good things happened.

Another example of bringing the "A" game occurred when I was flying as a United 727 Captain in 1996. The flight was Denver to Omaha on a Boeing 727. We were at cruise altitude of 37,000 feet about 110 miles west of Omaha. On a clear night in March, we started our descent into Omaha. As soon as I pushed the nose down to begin the descent on autopilot, a red light on the front instrument panel lit up to indicate low hydraulic pressure to the elevators that control the airplane's pitch. The autopilot immediately disconnected as it should, and I started hand flying. Looking back over my right shoulder at the flight engineers panel, I confirmed we had a total A-system hydraulic failure.

Bob, my flight engineer, also echoed it and shut off both A-system hydraulic pumps.

I handed the airplane over to Mark, my first officer, who already had the communication radios. From memory, we did the first items on the checklist for this particular hydraulic system failure. We already had clearance to descend, but we needed to continue to a lower altitude because of some aerodynamic flying restrictions regarding altitude and speed in the case of this type of hydraulic failure. I started to work with Bob on the checklist. We still had two other hydraulic systems that were working, and the airplane was flying just fine although with some reduced capacity.

I asked Mark to declare an emergency to air traffic control, so we could then do whatever we needed to meet the emergency. After we assessed the tasks at hand, we prioritized them. First, we flew the airplane. Then we handled the first part of the emergency. Finally, we planned how to handle the rest of the tasks before us. I contacted our dispatcher in Chicago, and he patched in an aircraft maintenance expert to help us handle the hydraulic failure. The A-system was responsible for the primary flap and landing gear extension. We could extend the wing flaps using an alternate electrical method. The flaps had to be extended so we could fly at a lower speed for a safe landing. We could extend the landing gear manually from the cockpit by using a hand crank. The cockpit floor had three small doors about the size of post cards that could be opened up to reveal a receptacle for a hand crank.

By a system of cables, we used the hand crank to unlock the landing gear so that it could free fall into position using its own weight. We informed our dispatcher of our situation. I told him that we should be able to handle everything normally. I also asked him to put the local emergency vehicles on alert and have them position themselves about two-thirds of the way down the longest runway.

The wind was favorable to use the runway landing to the northwest, which happened to be the longest. We would be landing with less-than normal flaps, so our touchdown speed would be about 20 miles per hour faster than normal. After landing, we would probably not have nose-wheel steering, and we would need to be towed clear of the runway to the gate. The dispatcher agreed to notify all concerned and asked if we needed anything else. I said no and that I would call him on the phone again after we arrived at the gate.

I called the Chief "A" flight attendant to the cockpit for a face-to-face briefing. As I explained the situation to him, I asked that all the flight attendants be on the lookout for anything strange going on with the airplane. They were our eyes and ears back there. I assured him we were expecting a normal landing and a tow into the gate. We might be a little late because of the extra time it was going to take to get our jobs done up here. If conditions got worse in a hurry, we would discuss further actions then.

He went to brief the other flight attendants before I made an announcement to the passengers. Then while I made an announcement to the passengers explaining the situation, Mark was descending the plane into the correct position for the next set of procedures. We needed to start extending the flaps electrically. This took some extra time, and we leveled off at 10,000 feet and made some large circles southwest of Omaha.

Then we were ready to extend the landing gear manually. The nose gear was first. Holding the flight manual, I read to Bob while he got out the hand crank. He pushed his engineer seat forward to expose the doors for the three hand crank receptacles, one for the nose landing gear and one for each of the main landing gears. He put the crank in for the nose gear and started to turn.

We were to follow a series of instructions to crank one way, then another to allow the cables to do their thing to open the gear doors, free fall the gear under its own weight, then lock it into place. Almost immediately, we got a light indicating that the nose gear was unlocked. We could hear a rush of wind in the cockpit from the nose gear doors opening. We were used to hearing this noise during normal operations. This time it was especially sweet to know that we had a nose gear down. Bob continued cranking more to lock the gear into place, and we had a green light indicating it was down and locked safely.

Next was the right main gear. Again, almost immediately after Bob started cranking, we got a red light on the forward panel indicating that the main gear doors were not locked closed. We are supposed to wait for a few seconds to let the gear doors fully open and be out of the way so that when we unlocked the main gear, it would fall out of the wheel well into place. We waited. Then Bob started to crank again to release the up-lock. The crank would not move.

I asked Bob about that, and he said he should push harder. For some reason, the crank and cable system was not moving the gear up-lock. Bob said he was afraid if he pushed too hard that he might break the crank. I asked him to try the other main gear. We got the door to open, no problem, just like the other one. When it came to unlocking the gear up-lock, it would not move either. We needed some help.

This was not going smoothly anymore. Calling dispatch, I asked to get maintenance on the line again for help. After explaining what we had, maintenance suggested that we fool the airplane into being on the ground by pulling some circuit breakers, then using the B-system hydraulics to force the gear down. The problem with that was the B-system was responsible for our primary brakes. Since we had a leak in the A-system, we could use the B-system pressure to get the gear down; however, the risk was that, if something went wrong, I might lose all my brakes except an emergency one-time brake application. That sounded pretty risky to me.

Then maintenance remarked that it might take up to 40 pounds of pressure on the crank to release the up-lock for the gear. That gave me an idea. I asked Bob to get on the floor and use his feet and legs to push against the crank. I was willing to have Bob break the cable and the crank to get the wheels down. I did not want to land with partial gear up—that would be bad. The ensuing evacuation would probably hurt people as well as damage the airplane further.

I wanted more wheels down. Bob pushed hard again and then we heard a pop. He got the up-lock to release. The right main gear fell into place and the light showed green. Bob continued to crank and lock the gear into place. Now he had some experience, and we continued the checklist on the other gear. He pushed hard again with his legs while sitting on the floor of the cockpit. We got the same result, and now three green lights on the forward panel indicated that all the landing gear was down and locked safely into place.

I told dispatch that we were now good to land and would call them when we were safely on the ground. Mark was still flying and handling the radio. I asked that we head for the airport and we could brief the remaining items before landing. Bob and I finished up the last few checklist items and prepared for the approach.

I took over flying for the landing and made a visual approach and a landing to the northwest. It was an uneventful landing. We regained enough hydraulic fluid during the gear extension to get our nose-wheel steering back. I was able to taxi to the gate under our own power while the fire trucks and emergency vehicles followed us to the gate. We were about ten minutes late. Some of the passengers were expecting a little more excitement since this was not long after the United 232 crash in Sioux City Iowa where a DC-10 lost all the hydraulics. I was glad that it seemed to be anti-climactic. I called dispatch from the Omaha operations and thanked them for their help. Later, we found out that the problem was a leak in one of the elevator control units.

About a week later, I was in Newark. Stopping by the maintenance office there, I asked a mechanic about the statement that we could use 40 pounds of pressure on the crank. In the training simulator, we practice these scenarios, and they can adjust the pressures any way they want. The maintenance manual that the mechanic was reading from pertained to a periodic check of this cable system for manual extension. Our particular airplane probably had not had that system exercised for some time (although within legal limits), so it was pretty stiff. As a pilot, I would have liked to have known about the possibility of using 40 pounds of pressure on the crank in case of emergency. It was not in our training or in our flight manual.

I wrote the required report on the incident and asked the fleet management of the Boeing-727 that the additional information be included in our training and our manuals. Both Mark, my first officer, and Bob, my second officer, were called into the flight office. We were all commended for our work. Shortly afterward, the Chicago Chief Pilot asked me if I would be willing to train other captains and first officers on this airplane. I agreed. I love to teach what I have learned. If someone else can gain from my experience, then we all win.

I was given additional training for the job of being a line-check airman. My job was to fly a regular schedule and, while doing so, train other captains and first officers to fly the B-727. After a pilot goes to our Denver flight training center to learn about the airplane systems and fly the simulator for about month, he gets released to fly with a line-check airman to finish the training in real-line operations. If I was training a new co-pilot, I would occupy my normal captain seat. If I was training a new captain, I would occupy the copilot's seat. Line-check airmen are the final filter following training before someone is released to fly. I did that for about five years until I moved up to the 757/767 fleet.

I have been asked to teach in every airplane I have flown since then. I declined the 757/767 but agreed after flying the 747 for a year to teach in that airplane again. I was a line-check airman for about three years on the 747. It is interesting to me how certain events can be perceived on the surface as being bad, but in a longer-term retrospective, they can be doorways to better things. The experience of dealing with this hydraulic failure helped cement things for me regarding what I am good at and what I love to do. Other people were able to see that as well, so it led to teaching at United.

Because I brought my "A" game to my training as a pilot, I was able to produce good results under difficult circumstances. I trained to be focused and disciplined to handle the emergency. Because I was always looking to improve my knowledge and help others, it was natural that I was asked to be part of the top 5% of United Airlines pilots by becoming a line-check airman.

CHAPTER WISDOM
Being disciplined enough to bring my "A" game to everything I do sets up the best outcomes.

CHAPTER 16

NUTRITION

If you want to fly, you must put jet fuel in the jet engine. I make about a hundred decisions per day that directly affect my health and thereby my performance. Many of those decisions relate to fuel—meaning food. I seek to keep my nutrition in proper balance. A great many books on the subject of nutrition have been published, and I am not an expert on it, but I know what works for me. I am going to make general recommendations rather a specific dietary plan. Here is what I do on a general basis.

I tried a lot of different things until I found what works for me. Everyone is different, and we are all constantly changing. I know that my needs and desires change over time. As a moving target, I keep shooting and striving for balance.

As a general rule, I eat just before a workout. When I am properly fueled, I will not run out of gas during the workout. My workouts usually last a couple of hours, so having a full tank before starting is important. Some people need time after consuming food before they can comfortably be active. As a result, they do not like to eat immediately before exercising. For me, it is not a problem. I have learned how to eat right before training. Try experimenting and adjust to what works for you. A breakfast that has some good protein for lasting energy as well as some good carbohydrates to fuel the muscles and brain will help. In addition, a balance of good fats will help the body to absorb the proteins.

During a workout if I run out of fuel, my muscles will start eating themselves to provide the necessary energy to keep going. I can usually tell if that is happening because I will notice an ammonia-like smell about me and in my sweat. Running out of fuel or getting dehydrated like this is a sure sign that I need to take in some food and water. For a short workout, only water is necessary. However, when I do anything extended, I need some regeneration fuel. Energy gels, energy chews, goop, Power Bars, Clif Bars, bananas, or just grape juice all work.

To provide an example of the type of fueling I do, I will explain my morning routine for a skating workout. I wake up at 5 am and start with some coffee. Then after a shower, I have a good breakfast of either oatmeal mixed with walnuts for protein (so I don't run out of energy mid morning) or eggs. I am out the door by 6:30 am to drive about 90 minutes to the rink, drinking more coffee. I then start my pre-ice warm-up routine, usually by drinking a combo of grape juice and water (mostly water) for hydration and energy. Just before getting on the ice about 9 am, I eat a banana. (Since it has been two-and-a-half hours since breakfast, I need to fuel again.) Through trial and error, I have learned that if I don't fuel again, I will run out of gas on the ice (not good). I like to drink a water and grape juice mix while on the ice for the next 90 minutes for hydration and energy.

After the ice workout, I cool down on the bike and then do a good stretch. After or during the stretch, I will eat another banana. Then I eat lunch. If I do not eat again within 15-30 minutes after finishing my cool down, my muscles will start eating themselves to resupply the used-up glycogen (the main way glucose is stored in the human body). This would be very counterproductive! During the drive home, I continue to hydrate.

If I am not disciplined about food, then it is like taking two steps forward and one step back. Because I am putting a great deal of work into my training, eating needs to be productive, not destructive. The goal of moving constantly forward is the basic framework I work within. However, sometimes special circumstances require me to adapt. Nothing is ever perfect. Sometimes, I must settle for than less than ideal circumstances and plan as best as possible.

Another thing to consider is nutrition and competition. Everyone reacts differently to competition. Some people cannot eat at all before a competition, and some people are the opposite. Figure out what works for you. Test it too. I remember my first triathlon vividly. This triathlon started with a half-mile swim in a pool, then a 20-mile bike, then finally a 5-mile run. A water bottle on my bike was filled with Gatorade, and I drank some before getting off the bike and starting the run portion of the race. I thought it would be a good time to do some replenishing of fluids, electrolytes, and sugar. I took in a few mouthfuls, then I started running. After a short time, my stomach started cramping. I ran doubled over in pain for the first two miles of the 5-mile run. I had done no testing beforehand of how I might respond to Gatorade, and I reacted badly.

Now I test and experiment with anything I am going to use nutritionally in connection with my training and racing. Trying different things and seeing how they work, talking to other athletes to find out what works for them helps me too. Then I can modify and fine-tune my routine. It is also very important not to change anything when you are approaching a competition or performance. Stick with what works, and don't make major changes close to important events.

In the off-season and during a taper leading up to a major competition, I must use a different eating plan. I am still active but I am not putting in the training volume, so there is no need to continue the uptake of massive amounts of calories. Listening to my body's needs and what it is telling me is the key.

As I eat better, my body and mind become more sensitive to good and bad foods. The same is true of supplements. I used to think that I needed extra protein in my diet as a supplement. I did not think I could maintain an adequate level of protein intake to continue to build my muscles.

In the summer of 2008, we did a nutritional analysis. First, we did a body composition analysis of muscle and fat to see where I stood. Then a workout analysis to see where the energy was going. Then a food diary for seven days that included everything I ate, including supplements, vitamins, etc. While I was doing the food diary, I flew a three-day trip to Frankfurt, Germany, so the diary included some airline food and body clock changes. Then we sent all the data to our nutritional analyst in Argentina. The results were very interesting. The analysis showed that I was getting all the nutrition I needed from my food alone. This was as much of a validation of how Maripat was feeding me and our food decisions as anything else. Nothing extra was needed, so the supplements were actually hurting me. The nutritional expert recommended stopping the supplements. I agreed and have not used them since.

Looking back, I realized I had been having some issues with my bladder, kidneys, liver, and prostate before I stopped the supplements. When I was eating poorly, the supplements worked ok. When I started eating better food, my body no longer needed the supplements and started to dump them into various organs. I was seeing an acupuncturist at the time, and he confirmed what I was going through. We used acupuncture and some Chinese herbs to help flush the extra supplements from my system. It took about a year for my body to get back into a better balance. I am healthier now than ever.

My nutritional goals are simple. I strive to give myself the best chance possible at optimum health. What, when, and how much I put in my mouth has a great bearing and influence on my health, my well-being, and my performance. By sticking with what works, listening to my body, making appropriate changes, and always treating myself like an athlete, I perform better in all areas of my life.

If I am having trouble with my food intake, I must look at the thoughts I have about food and my relationship with food first. By doing this, then I can get a handle on what is motivating me. What conscious and unconscious barriers are there to my progress? Cultural programming might also be driving my decisions. For example, while I was growing up, my parents told us to always clean our plates at meals. The reason they gave was that children were starving in China, so we should not let food go to waste. I no longer have that scarcity mentality regarding food. There is plenty of food, and I no longer have to finish everything on my plate. I am willing to take responsibility for that because I am the only one living in my body. I am the only expert on how full I am and what I need for food intake.

Stress affects my eating habits, and it is constant and inevitable. How I respond to stress through eating is my choice. Sometimes I feel it, and sometimes I don't. Whether I feel its negative effects or not is usually contingent upon a host of factors. When I am in a good place physically, mentally, psychologically, and spiritually, I can weather almost anything stressful. When I am not in in a good place, I can view food as a drug that eases the pain. I watch out for cravings and look for warning signs of getting off my eating plan or straying from my intention.

That's not to say that all cravings are bad. Sometimes cravings are ok because they are my body's way of telling me something. If a banana looks particularly good to me, my brain is telling me I need it. There is probably something in the banana I lack, so I should eat it. Paying attention to my thoughts and feelings, as well as my cravings is the key.

CHAPTER WISDOM

Proper nutrition sets up the body and mind to do great work. Discipline with nutrition will pay great dividends, internal and external.

PART THREE

CHAPTER 17

COACHING AND THE COACH-ATHLETE RELATIONSHIP

Mirrors are amazing devices. In my physical training, my coach and I frequently use mirrors to adjust my body position. Yet, I use mirrors in a figurative way as well. A coach is like a mirror. When we can see ourselves through the eyes of a coach, change becomes possible and probable. In contrast, trying to be my own expert has been disastrous for me. Selecting someone who can help me along my path is very important. Such a guide needs to be a good fit. I have had several coaches in my life and will no doubt have more. I trust that each coach who has come along has been the right one at the right time for my learning process.

The coach-athlete relationship needs to embody a certain synchronicity. Everyone puts out a certain vibration, and I've learned that following my gut and being sensitive to that feeling when picking a coach is very important. This will help the relationship grow, flourish, and be good for both of us. That is the goal in a perfect world. The real world is very different, but we must continually strive to obtain what we need.

The first question to ask when considering coaching is, "Am I coachable?" This will be a rudimentary question for some and a very difficult one for others. I have been at opposite ends of this spectrum in different parts of my life. As a youngster, I attended a few summer camps to learn about skating and training. I had a correspondence relationship with a couple of coaches. One was Dutch and one was Norwegian. We wrote letters that took weeks to deliver. By learning as much as I could, I became my own expert. Because I developed some hard and fast rules for my training, I became unshakable in most of my ideas and was not very coachable at the time.

Years later as a masters skater, I realized I had a lot of knowledge and expertise. I had wisdom based on my life experiences and was an expert on many things, but there was still some blockage where coaching was concerned. I was not moving forward as well as I could, so I accepted that I could not see myself as well as a coach could. I was becoming open to new ideas about how to do things, and I was now ready to listen to a coach.

My current coach says that I am very coachable. To me, this means I am willing to hear what she has to say and try it to the best of my ability. I no longer feel that I have to justify what I am doing, just try to do it differently. This attitude has taken a long time to adopt. My ability to do so is connected to my improved self-esteem. The better we feel about ourselves, the easier it is to change. That's what being coachable is all about.

The coach-athlete relationship is similar to a family relationship in many ways. In order for it to work well and flourish, it must be given the priority of just below family.

Proximity is important in any relationship. Long distances are possible in coach-athlete relationships, but they can be hard. There is no substitute for looking into someone's eyes and seeing their body language to get the feedback that a coach needs to make adjustments. Having a coach who can be on the scene is the best arrangement. When you are willing to do the work of finding and fostering a coach-athlete relationship, the benefits outweigh the costs every time.

Communication between a coach and an athlete is the only way an athlete can make progress. In order for the communication to be effective, I must be absolutely honest with myself first, then with my coach. My career in aviation has helped me to see what effective communication can do. To pass on those lessons, I will explain what I know works for me in the coach-athlete relationship.

For effective communication to take place, people must follow some essential steps. First, the idea must be verbalized. This verbalization must be done in a constructive way. The next step is timing. The information must take place when the athlete is attentive. If my coach yells something at me when I am totally focused on my performance, hearing is impossible. As a dad and soccer coach, I remember never to shout anything to the boy with the ball during a game. Talking to the boys without the ball is more effective. In addition, if the athlete is alert and attentive, then he or she has a better chance of hearing what the coach is trying to get across.

Conversely, as an athlete, I need to pay attention to what my coach is trying to get across to me. There is no harm in saying, "Sorry, I could not hear you, say again?" or "What did you say? I could not listen till now."

But for true communication to take place, the people involved must have a meaningful exchange. As a coach, you want some insightful response back from your athlete. If my coach tries to convey a point of technique to me, then says "Do you understand?" and I respond with a yes or a nod, she has no way of telling whether any real ideas were exchanged. On the other hand, if I say something meaningful or insightful back or if I physically demonstrate understanding, my coach knows I absorbed her point.

To sum up, it is important to communicate clearly, honestly, and when the listener is available to really listen. Then make sure that something meaningful and insightful is the result of the exchange. Everyone communicates differently. It is up to me, as an athlete, to make sure that I effectively take in what my coach is trying to get across to me. It is in my interest to have a coach and my responsibility to make the relationship work.

My eyes can look only outside myself, both literally and figuratively. As I have noted before, a great quote about denial is, "Between me and you and me is only air, but between me and myself is a lifetime of denial." As I see the world through my filter, colored by my own experience and personality, things can get very cloudy. To see myself clearly in any mirror, I must wipe it off. Honesty is the tool with which I can wipe off the mirror. My coach can be a mirror, and so can others in my support network. When I see myself clearly as reflected in their mirrors, I can make the necessary adjustments to improve. Receiving the mirror of feedback from my coach, then making adjustments is how growth works best.

I try to pick the coach who has the expertise that I need. Different coaches have different areas of expertise. My needs change over time and so does my desire for expertise in different areas. No one coach has it all.

The qualities I look for in a coach are numerous. Is this coach willing to go to others to expand his or her expertise? Do I want to spend considerable time with this person? Do I want to spend my effort with this person? Do I like this coach as a person? Would I consider this person a friend if he or she was not my coach? For anyone choosing a coach, those are important questions to consider.

Coaches cost money. Everyone has to earn a living. If I am asking a coach to sacrifice time, then I must be willing to compensate for that time. A lot of people find it harder to talk about money than about sex. I have learned to talk about money and compensation to the extent necessary to prevent it from being an ongoing issue. If money is an unresolved issue, then anger and resentment will build. Anger and especially resentment will color the relationship and generally poison it if left unresolved. Everything regarding money must be out in the open, so it can be resolved quickly and leave no lasting effects, clouding the relationship and progress towards my goal.

After choosing a coach, I must respect that what I am given is proprietary information. If I pass my coach's techniques on to someone else, then I have given away something of value that she had worked hard on.

I have a rule about the learning process. The 10, 3, 1, teach rule. In order for me to learn something I must hear it 10 times, do it 3 times, mess it up once (so I know the cost of not doing it right), and finally teach it to someone else to really know it and own it.

PART THREE

As I learned to fly airplanes, this principle became readily apparent to me. I needed to hear a concept, idea, or task many times for it to sink in. I needed to repeat it at least three times to find the full range of a task, to see the boundaries, and then bring it back to center. By making a mistake, I get to see the consequences of not getting it right. (For safety, pilots in training make their mistakes in simulators, on monitored-flights, and in other controlled situations.) But to really own something, I must be able to pass it onto someone else.

As a beginning flight instructor early in my professional flying career, I learned that teaching can be a valuable lesson in itself. I had the tools of being a safe pilot, which I was to pass on to new students. In order to demonstrate and explain a task many different ways, to many different types of people with many different learning styles, I truly had to own what I was teaching. As a result, being a teacher cemented important concepts, tasks, and ideas much more firmly in my own mind. If I could explain an idea six different ways, then I understood it much better myself.

In a coaching environment, I must be willing to go through this process in reverse; as the student, I give back the insightful idea to my coach so she knows I got it. This is much deeper than just repeating what I get from my coach or just showing what I can do. Instead, I must know all the aspects of learning something new.

Another factor in a coaching relationship is availability. I have almost daily contact with my coach. If I am traveling on the other side of the planet, such regular communication can be tough to maintain. If I want a lot of contact, then I must put in the work to maintain it. How important is this really? I will ask another question. How important am I? Am I worth it? If I have gone to all this trouble to hire a coach, why would I not use my coaching resource to my full advantage to further my goals?

In the course of any relationship, the participants encounter forks in the road. By entering into a coach-athlete relationship, I have already asked for something. This is a contract. All relationships have spoken and unspoken contracts. Some of the unspoken contracts may be of a cultural nature. It is essential to keep unspoken contracts to a minimum. Such openness may be hard, but sometimes we must uncover those unspoken contracts to clarify the landscape. For example when Nancy Swider-Peltz, Sr. and I started working together, she was apprehensive about spending too much time with me. She had higher-priority athletes (Olympians and her own children) to coach, and she was worried I might ask too much of her and pull her away from them. I sensed this right away and was able to clear the air about my respect for her priorities. I also took full responsibility for my work and the results of my performance. I encouraged her to take credit for what I achieved but none of the blame if I didn't. The beauty for me of exposing these issues is that doing so created a clear path ahead. This sets up the situation of asking for what I need and for what I want. The benefit of this coaching relationship is for me, no one else, so I need to feel enough self-worth to ask for these things.

My coach cannot read my mind. I must ask for what I need. I used to be afraid to ask for what I needed in a relationship because I might be turned down. Eventually, I realized that the fear was always worse than the consequences. Asking for what I need takes courage, but I know now that it is worth the risk. I have already spent a great deal of time and energy on my goals, why not take this step? When I take a risk, the rewards are usually greater than I could have imagined. Fear kept me from seeing any other solutions. When you come to a fork in the road, take one or the other path and keep moving. If it is the wrong fork, backtrack, take the other with complete confidence, and go faster than before.

Because of my coach's expertise and because she has been where I want to go, I trust her knowledge. Still, the final authority for decisions still lies with me.

I will use the example of being an airline captain. Federal Aviation regulations state that I am the final authority as to the operation of the aircraft I am commanding. I have at least one and sometimes three co-pilots, depending on the length of the flight. I can have up to seventeen licensed flight attendants, a licensed dispatcher, a licensed mechanic—all involved in some of the operation and decisions regarding the aircraft. I can create an environment for and actively solicit input, but I must still make the final decisions about how to operate the airplane.

If I have used the input from all interested parties and they feel like they have a voice and a stake in the outcome, then I will have their support for the course of action I ultimately choose and am responsible for. Everyone is then pulling on the same end of the rope, and we move forward smoothly. By periodically asking the question, "How are we doing?" then I can solicit more input and refine the path. In a coach-athlete relationship, it is important to be absolutely clear about where I want to go, but the final decisions rest with me.

CHAPTER WISDOM

Be coachable, find and foster a coach-athlete relationship.

CHAPTER 18

TRAINING I: GENERAL TRAINING PRINCIPLES

One of my early memories of growing up is doing crazy things. Little did I know that this kind of play was the beginning of my training. Bart and I were probably about 6 and 8 years old at the time. We had skateboards, the kind that were about 2 feet long with metal roller skating wheels bolted to the bottom. Our driveway from the house to the sidewalk was sloped slightly, so we could get a little speed rolling downhill, maybe a fast walking speed. After mastering the skateboard on the driveway, we tried some other stuff. Bart liked hanging upside down on the monkey bars across the street in the park. When we started to go down the driveway on the skateboard in a handstand, it seemed like a logical progression from our other activities. This helped both of us to develop strength and balance early. Certainly, it helped Bart in his gymnastics career, and it also helped me in my balance for skating.

Making time to put in the work can be hard. I was asked the other day about how I find the time to train at this level. My answer was that I don't find the time, I make the time. This goes back to setting goals and priorities. Following through with a training plan is easier when I make the time. It has taken years to put myself into a job that allows blocks of time off to pursue my other passions. By carefully looking at our schedules, we can figure out ways to make time to pursue our goals and keep our priorities straight. We all have unexpected things come up in our lives that require us to put us off our training schedules. Adaptation with balance is the key to making progress.

Athletic training, in general, has two major parts: building the motor (strength, endurance, cardio), and then developing the technique to apply it. My knowledge and expertise has been developed by trial and error and by talking to other athletes on similar paths. The lessons I've learned in training may be actively applied to other parts of life. My training regimen has eight parts.

Practicing the sport

Warm-up, cool-down, volume, and intensity

Strength work

Cardiovascular work

Periodization

Stretching

Mental training

Rest

The first part is to practice my craft—in this case, speed skating. I can skate on the ice (when available), rollerblade, do imitation skating on dry land, or use a slide-board. The second part is the related principles of warm-up, cool-down, volume, and intensity. The third part is to build strength by weight training. The fourth part is building the cardiovascular component to supply my muscles with oxygen and nutrients. I can build my heart and lung capacity by running, cycling, swimming, etc. The fifth part is the principle of periodization in managing the training load through the training season. The sixth part is stretching. I can do yoga or any type of dynamic and static stretching. I like to use yoga as a separate workout to promote flexibility and mind-fullness. The seventh part is the mental training aspect, which is a separate exercise using visualization and rehearsal as well as an active application during my training. The last part is rest, active as well as passive. Active rest is necessary to promote recovery. Passive is just like it sounds, stopping and doing nothing, physically and mentally.

By applying the general principles of athletic training to anything that requires commitment, dedication, perseverance, and discipline, you can achieve extraordinary results.

Practicing my sport

When I started skating as a youngster, what attracted me was the sport itself and the joy of doing it. We must all remember our roots and our early motivation to get us through the hard work of training. When I skate and race, I put everything together: strength, endurance, technique, cardio work, mental training, everything. This is my toughest test as well as my best barometer of progress. Here is where the skate meets the ice.

There is nothing natural about speed skating. It is a purely learned activity that requires a fair amount of strength. Because of the strength required, skaters do not have the luxury of a lot of repetition. In order to skate technically well, a skater cannot be too tired. When I get tired, my technique suffers and thereby my speed.

In the United States, we have long track ice at two indoor 400-meter ovals about six months of the year from September through March. In Olympic years, we might have ice a month or so longer. It is important to skate, but it is also important to do off-ice imitation skating in the form of inline skating, dry-land training, and slide-board. I am constantly refining my technique to get the maximum speed. When I skate, I have several types of workouts. One workout is endurance skating: many laps at low intensity concentrating on technique and efficiency. Another workout is at race pace for short distances, typically 400 to 600 meters. We have several types of interval workouts as well, which intersperse hard skating with periodic rests. Then we have sprint workouts where we go all out hard for very short distances, interspersed with long rests. The goal is to refine our technique on the ice, since there is no true substitute, while simulating the different parts of racing. My coach is usually on hand for these sessions to direct and modify training as I go, as well as help to refine technique.

In whatever sport you are engaged in, you must learn to apply some amount of technique. Even something as seemingly simple as cycling can benefit because you can learn more efficient ways of pedaling. In speed skating, technique is extremely important. The faster I want to go, the better I must skate technically. This means striving for great body positioning and the most efficient way to push into the ice. If I have poor technique, I will skate slowly. When I improve my ability to apply my motor to the ice, I go faster and longer with the same effort.

Warm-up, Cool-down, Volume, and Intensity

I learned some of my most important work ethics from my high school cross-country and track coach, Patrick Savage. He showed me what hard work was all about. We would warm up with a 2-mile jog, then stretch warm muscles. Then the hard work would come. After that, we would always cool down with another 2-mile jog and stretch. This core principle of warming up and cooling down still shapes all my workouts today. As a masters athlete, if I need to cut out anything, it will not be in the warm up or cool down. Cutbacks will always be in the body of the workout. When I am doing active rest and recovery, only a warm up and cool down are necessary.

High school was where I first became aware of what training volume was all about. Before then, I did not have very much reference for training volume. I knew that I needed to work out nearly everyday. In fact, I recently came across some old training diaries. At one time when I was 15 years old, I had sixteen workouts scheduled for the week. That was two workouts a day, seven days a week, plus an additional workout twice a week. The volume of training I did as a youth was incredible. During the warm summer vacations, I could get in three workouts per day.

Making a good warm up and a good cool down a priority is essential. When I don't follow this plan, I pay for it with soreness and possible injury. I have a couple of training rules that I do not break. If I do, then I will pay the price. The first rule is never stretch cold muscles. If I stretch a cold rubber band, I might break it. The same is true of muscles. The first thing to do during a warm up is to bring the muscles up to an operating temperature. I start walking, running, or cycling first, slowly of course, then increase gradually as my muscles heat up. I usually start with about 10 minutes of stationary bike or running about 8 minutes.

The important thing is to get a little sweat going and a heart rate around 120 beats per minute. Then I do about 10 minutes of dynamic stretching. Dynamic stretching is stretching with movement. An example might be where I take a step forward and pull one knee to my chest, then alternate with the other leg as I step forward. Swinging my arms in big circles to get full range of motion would be another dynamic stretch.

Next I spend about 10 minutes with some static stretches. An example of static stretches would be lying on the ground and bending forward touching my toes with my fingers to stretch the hamstrings (back of the legs and butt). During these stretches, the purpose is only to get the full range of motion. After the workout is when I work on increasing my flexibility. Static stretches are typically held for about 10 seconds.

My warm-up period lasts about 30 minutes. Then I am fully ready to do some hard work because my muscles are flexible through full range of motion and are up to a good working temperature. After the bulk of the workout, I spend more time cooling down by cycling for 10 minutes or running at a slow pace with hardly any load or effort. The purpose is to speed the flushing of waste products from the muscles. If I finish the hard part of my workout and then stop immediately, my muscles will still be building up the waste products of my work. If I don't take the time to flush them out, I will get sore and stiff. I have also broken down my muscles to a degree during the workout. This creates some inflammation. Cooling down with an easy jog, a walk, or a spin on the bike will help flush my muscles of waste, calm the inflammation, and speed recovery.

After a cool down, I spend some extra time with static stretching. This is where I can do injury prevention. Once I have warm muscles that are very pliable, I can increase my flexibility better than at any other time. During these stretches, I want to hold each pose for about 30 seconds. During the cool down, holding and pressing the stretch will increase flexibility.

The volume of workouts I was able to build up to as an athlete over the age of 50 is incredible. The key is increasing gradually. I know I am a "speed" skater, so it may seem contradictory that I say to go slowly, but by increasing my workload slowly, I get the best results. A few of my injuries were directly attributable to increasing my workload too fast. The best way for me to avoid doing that is to keep track of what I am doing—a record of what I have done and what I plan to do in any workout. Gauging my increases accurately gives the best chance at success. I do not trust my memory.

Listening to my body is essential in this endeavor. I also keep track of how I am feeling before, during, and after each workout. Some people keep a diary or journal of their feelings and look back through it to see what has been happening for perspective. My first experience with hard training was as a teenager. My concept was that if I trained harder than everybody else, then I would be faster and I would be successful. That is true to a degree, but it's not the whole picture. Building the motor is only part of the equation.

You may be asking, "If I have to start slowly and increase slowly, will I ever reach my goals?" My answer is that if I can just take that first step today and come back for more tomorrow, then I am farther down the road. If I had gone overboard the first day and had to backtrack from injury, then I am no further toward my goal. Consistency is the key to a long journey.

Strength Training

Strength training is essential. I will not go into the benefits here because many books have been written and studies have been done on the benefits. For a speed skater, strength is essential. The benefits are numerous. I train very hard at developing my strength, which produces huge benefits. As a young man, I did weight training, but not as much as I do now. Strength training enhances and improves everything. One benefit is that I am a better runner because I am stronger; I run with better economy and efficiency, I play tennis better, swing a golf club better, etc.

Because of strength, I am able to apply my leg strength to the ice through a very strong core without compromising my lower back or being prone to injury. Strength and weight training has also helped me develop stronger connective tissue and bones. This helps to prevent injuries.

My strength work is one weight workout per week. I do about a dozen different exercises. I do only one for my legs and that is a leg press machine. I no longer use free weights. The chance of injury is high, and the benefit from free weights is negligible. I use machines that have a cam system that distributes constant stress through the full range of motion of the joint I am working. I do one set of 6 reps to failure. For example, on the leg press, I will extend up from the starting position of a 90-degree knee bend to almost straight in 10 seconds, then 10 seconds back down to 90 degrees again. I never fully extend or rest the weight so I am constantly under load. It takes 2 minutes to do 6 repetitions. Then I do three jumps to a bench about knee height two times and walk around for a couple of minutes before going onto the next machine. This exhausts the slow, medium, medium fast and fast twitch muscle fibers all at the same time. It takes about a week to recover. I keep track of what I have done and increase the next week. I make progress every week and I am stronger than ever.

Cardiovascular Work

Anytime I move, my heart starts raising its rate to keep up with my workload. Virtually, all of my training has a cardiovascular component to it. A couple of times a week, I do some pure cardio work to train my heart and lungs. When I am on the ice, I can consider it a strength and cardio workout. Even skating slow laps requires a great deal of strength, and my heart rate increases to a high level before long.

I do two types of cardio work, mostly on a stationary bike. One type of workout is interval training. The other is extensive tempo. The difference is that interval training is of a higher intensity but with rest between the efforts. The extensive tempo training is doing something at a lower intensity but continuously for a longer time frame. An example of an interval workout would be running 400 meters pretty hard so that you are breathing heavily at the end, then resting by jogging 200 meters, then repeating. This was the workout we did when I was in high school as a freshman running cross country, and we repeated this cycle about 12 times in a workout. I can still do this today. It takes about an hour to do this part of the workout. An extensive tempo workout would be running for the same hour but at a slower pace continuously.

Both types of workouts have benefits for your heart and lungs. To get the full benefits of cardio training, you should use both methods each week. Many times, my coach schedules an extensive tempo bike workout in the evening after an intense morning workout on the ice to help flush out the byproducts that built up earlier. This way I get the benefit of the flush as well as the cardio training for my heart. Swimming is also a great non-weight-bearing exercise that can help with heart and lung capacity. I can do tempo, intervals, or recovery work by swimming.

Periodization

Periodization is like a flight of stairs. The first level—which can be equated to any workload and any exercise—is the first step. Let's take the example of sit-ups. I can start out by doing so many of a certain type. Let's say that I am doing sit-ups twice a week. I keep track of the type of sit-ups and how many. The next week I increase the sit-ups. I can increase the sit-ups by a number of ways: I can increase the number I do by adding to a set or adding another set; I can decrease the rest time between sets; I can change the difficulty of sit-up to one that is inclined or one that incorporates weights. The important thing is to increase each week.

At a certain point we reach a plateau. Then it is important to change. I need rest and have to back off the intensity and volume for a couple of weeks. By just going through the motions for about a week, we are healing from the intense work. Then I can start to increase again. Now I can start up again just below where I took the break. By repeating this process of increasing, then easy, then increasing again, I become better and stronger overall in the long run and less prone to burnout and injury.

The concept of periodization also applies to the larger training cycle of a season and peak performance for a race. I train very hard so that I break down and rebuild stronger. This cycle can be used to achieve peak performance for a certain event. Approaching the important competition, I will cut down the volume of my work but maintain the intensity. By doing a lot more recovery and rest, I can approach the starting line rested and ready to push at maximum capacity. The length of the tapering of volume prior to the competition is usually in direct relation to the length of hard training leading up to the competition. I have found it is better to have too long a rest than not enough.

The concept of tapering training volume and intensity was foreign to me when I was young. That was why I burned out at age 19 and was unable to compete at the level I had trained and prepared for. I believed that the person who trained the hardest would win. I put everything I had into training all the way up to the competition with no rest. I was so tired that my technique suffered and my muscles were worn out, so I could not skate well at all. Now I know very well what the concept of tapering is and how to use it. Now I use the periodization process and tapering, and I plan my training to the utmost benefit.

Age is also a variable where tapering is concerned. My ability to recover is not as fast as that of younger skaters, so my taper must be a little longer. As I age, I have realized I can keep up with the younger skaters if I give myself a longer rest.

The whole idea of tapering for a major competition is that I should approach the starting line feeling totally rested and ready to go. In fact, compared to the training volume and intensity I maintained as a young man, I should feel like I am lazy and out of shape. That is when I race my fastest. A great deal of science supports all of this, and my own experience bears it out.

Stretching

Stretching has three major components and uses for me. The first is during my warm-up process. I never stretch cold muscles, ligaments, or tendons. I bring my body up to a warm temperature by jogging, biking, or fast walking, then I stretch to get full range of motion of my joints. I like to think of my muscles as rubber bands. If I stretch a cold rubber band, it might break; a warm one is more flexible. When stretching for range of motion, I will hold a pose for about 10 seconds. After my cool down, I will stretch again. This time I will hold my poses for 30 seconds. The purpose of this kind of stretch is to increase flexibility, promote recovery, and prevent injury. The last component is a workout designed just around stretching. Yoga is a great tool for me, so I try to do it weekly. Spending a whole hour stretching has benefits that go far beyond just flexibility and range of motion. Yoga can help me open up the connection from my head to my heart, help me be mind-full and calm, and get re-charged and re-centered.

Mental Training

Mental training has three aspects for me. The first is rehearsal and visualization. While I am learning a new skill, I need to rehearse and visualize a good process and outcome. As I make progress, I will continually rehearse whatever I am working on to reinforce what I have learned and to cement the neural connections in my brain and the links to my muscles. The second part is to make a list of positive affirmations to create the landscape of where I want to go. By creating this future picture of myself, I set up the conditions for me to live into the reality I have created. The third aspect is preparation for my competition. I will take the rehearsal and visualization and apply it to the competition at hand. This preparation starts weeks and sometimes years before and ends when I cross the finish line and stand on the podium. I have developed a routine for competition and a mantra that I repeat to myself as I approach the starting line. This is when I apply my mental training to get the most out of my physical preparation. During the race, I have control only of my execution; the physiology of my muscles is already set.

Rest

Rest is just what it says, rest from activity. Rest is either passive or active. There are many parts to rest. I will address them in different contexts. Normal training consists of a few different cycles. The largest context is the four-year Olympic cycle. The shift in focus will change from year to year as the Olympic year approaches. As I change and my goals change, so will my rest requirements change.

Within the Olympic cycle is the yearly cycle that every competitive athlete goes through. The yearly cycle must include periods of rest. I generally finish my competitive season in the middle of March. I then take at least six to eight weeks off of training. During this time, it is important to let my body and mind heal from the intense work I did over the past ten months or so. I take a break in many ways, like catching up on the things I have put off due to my competition and training schedule. I am less active physically; this is my winter. I let the field rest so it can produce again later with more abundance, just as farmers do for their crops. During this time, I can do a number of things. One thing I like to do is to continue a little very easy biking and stretching.

I do nothing intense, everything just for fun! When I was growing up, my parents stressed that I should learn my sport the best I could, but also learn sports I could do for life. For example, I learned to play golf and tennis, and I still enjoy them today. Doing other sports will help me be a better skater because I will have a better, more rounded foundation to draw from. The important principle in active rest is to keep the intensity low. When I am ready to start the training cycle over again, my body and mind will tell me. I cannot force the issue! Starting back too soon or too fast will cause me to burn out again or get injured.

Because I am used to a lot of physical activity, stopping cold turkey will throw me off. It is still important to be active, just not as much and without any real intensity. My body needs the rest, and I must give in to it or suffer in the long run.

One very important element in my training regimen is periodic massage. Muscles need help to recover. One way to assist in recovery is massage. In order to keep up my training volume, I need recovery. The more quickly I recover, the more training volume and intensity are possible. My race results directly correspond to my training volume and intensity. I do self-massage and get great results. I use foam rollers, my hands, and a stick roller for self massage. I also hire a professional masseuse sometimes. I have a pretty good understanding of my own body and what it is going through, but using a trained massage professional brings another helpful dimension to my recovery.

Usually a massage therapist can find hot spots that I was not even aware of. After the therapist has found these spots and worked on them, my body then spends less energy on a "wound" and more energy on my general recovery. Ideally, a massage every week would be the best for me, but that is not always possible or practical.

Another tool that I use to gauge whether I am training to an optimum level is ithlete. I heard about ithlete from a fellow speed skater, researched it, and decided that this was something that might help me decide when to go hard and when to back off on my training. The ithlete device is an application on my smart phone that uses a receiver and my polar heart monitor to measure heart rate variability. I take a measurement immediately after waking in the morning to gauge my readiness to train hard that day. Illness and stress in my life will give me low numbers and tell me that I need rest or to train more easily that day. It reflects all of my life factors, including a very high training load. In the past, I would train right through these times, and my racing suffered as a result. This tool can give me physical feedback and validates the feelings I get when I am on track or overtrained.

When I look at my monthly training plan, I must plan my rest accordingly. Through trial and error, I have found that after working hard for three weeks I must reduce my intensity and volume and do an active rest week. I will decrease my intensity and volume for a week, so that I may avoid burn out or injury. In the weekly plan, I also include a rest day, usually Sunday. During the week, I will space my intense training out so that there are no two days in a row without a rest or recovery day. For instance, skating is like doing a hard weight workout. I will not do weights one day, then skate the next. That would be counterproductive. I will do a cardio bike recovery workout, swimming, or yoga in between skating and weights. In training, as in life, keeping everything in balance is the key to making progress.

CHAPTER WISDOM

Build the motor and learn how to apply it to your endeavor. Utilize the principles of practice, warm-up, cool-down, volume, intensity, strength, cardio, periodization, stretching, mental training, and rest.

PART THREE

CHAPTER 19

TRAINING II: INJURIES AND PREVENTION

As far as injuries are concerned, my policy is prevention, prevention, prevention. I observe a number of basic principles when it comes to injury prevention and management. The first is listening to my body and learning to respond to it quickly and appropriately. Every time I train, I create some injury. Through the work I do, I deliberately break down my body. Our bodies respond by rebuilding themselves stronger than before. By managing minor, self-inflicted injuries (my training), I will grow stronger over time. Building up tolerance by increasing very slowly is crucial. For example, if I am going to run a marathon this year, I would need to have a base to start from. I would need to demonstrate consistent mileage without injury on the kinds of running surface I would be training and racing on. Injuries generally occur because the body is not responding well to the increase or not recovering quickly enough to do the increased volume.

Using the proper equipment can help prevent injuries.

Analyzing body mechanics is another important tool for injury prevention. Using a professional trainer can be indispensable in this area. A trainer can show me how to set up a stationary bike to avoid injuring myself over the long term. A trainer can show me the proper way to lift weights to avoid injury and to gain the most benefit. Using a lower weight with good mechanics and low injury potential is more productive than using a higher weight that might look better to my friends but risk injury. Competing with others in the gym while lifting weights will be counterproductive in the long run. In fact, I apply this principle to almost all physical activity.

Longevity as an athlete is dependent on body mechanics. To increase my chances of a long, productive life, I treat myself as a finely tuned athlete at maximum performance. Poor body mechanics can set me up for injuries—sometimes quickly, sometimes slowly over time. It is up to me. Using proper technique, for whatever activity, is essential to perform efficiently and to prevent injury. I believe in getting expert advice on as many of my activities as possible so as not to shortchange myself with an injury.

Goals then come into play. If I cannot increase my workload as quickly as I want because it would possibly cause an injury, then I must revise my goals. I may need to scale back to run a half marathon this year and a full marathon next year. This would be realistic.

I am not in the results business. I must keep moving my feet and trusting that the results are what they are. This includes injuries. If I really believe I am exactly in the place where I am supposed to be, then the lesson for me is waiting in whatever process I am engaged in. There will always be a timely solution and a gift from the issue. With this in mind, if I do sustain an injury, I can try many different solutions for my recovery. I know that being proactively involved in the process will help me to heal as quickly as possible.

Poor nutrition, unrealistic goals, misplaced priorities, uncontrolled ego—each of these can play a part in causing injuries. When an injury occurs, look at all the factors that surround it. Have I tried my own solutions? Is my injury beyond my help? Do I need a professional?

The acronym RICE stands for rest, ice, compression, and elevation. This is the rule of first aid to follow immediately after an injury. After the initial shock wears off, I can then evaluate what to do next.

When I am injured, I have a whole host of resources to draw from. First is myself. I am the only true expert on my body. No else lives in my body or my head but me. Am I getting out of my own way? When analyzing a situation involving injury, I must stick with the facts as they are, not as I would like them be. No drama or minimizing. What kind of pain is it, and how is it affecting me?

PART THREE

I am not best judge of myself, so I use people around me to provide a mirror to see myself more clearly. For example, when I walked into my physical therapist's office not too long ago, she told me within 10 seconds that I looked tired and asked me what was wrong. Because I was wearing my fatigue on the outside, she could plainly evaluate me and provide feedback.

Every injury teaches me a lesson. Protecting something that is weak only makes it weaker. Many times, a physical symptom is a manifestation of a deeper emotional issue that is surfacing and crying out to be dealt with. The underlying issue may not be evident for some time, but it is always there for me. Everything happens for a reason, and it is my job to figure out the lesson. Sometimes God is telling me to slow down, to change my thinking, to be more sensitive, or to be there for someone else. To think about the higher purpose, recognize it, accept it, and act upon it is the key.

It is important to create, attract, and foster people around me to give the feedback for change. Having a network of healing professionals—with whom I am absolutely honest about my history, wants, needs, and goals—is essential. Obtaining the information and treatment needed to move on from my injury is the goal.

Accidents do happen, but when they do, I try to remember the following saying: "Pain is inevitable, suffering is optional." My first reaction to pain isn't important. What matters is the response that I choose. If I can put on the pause button and choose my response to a situation—by looking at my circumstances, making judgments, and using the tools at my disposal—then I can move on from there in a conscious way. I may not know what the outcome will be, but I trust that everything will be OK. By creating that environment, then I have a better chance of living into a happy, free, injury-prevention, accident-free life. I know that I cannot avoid all injuries and accidents, but if I can respond appropriately to the challenges that come up, then I can turn knowledge into wisdom.

The process of an injury and healing will result in changed expectations. When I had knee surgery in 2009, I could have driven myself crazy with worry about how it was going to affect my racing season. However, spending a lot of emotional energy trying to figure out something impossible to predict is a waste. So I took it one day at a time, telling myself that the whole situation was going to work itself out anyway. I focused on doing my part, not looking too far out in front, and enjoying the ride. I believe there is a bigger picture and larger meaning in injury and recovery. I try to find a larger meaning and see where accidents and injuries can open new doors that would not have been available to me before. Accidents and injuries force me to look at things differently and help me gain new perspectives and find new roads ahead. Remaining open to life lessons in the throes of a crisis is not so easy, but with time and practice, it becomes easier. Do I look for silver linings? You bet. Conversely, if I look to an injury as a limitation, arguing for it, then I have accepted that limitation as mine! That is my choice, my responsibility, and my accountability.

After an injury that requires some time off, starting up again can be tough. Falling prey to two types of thinking are possible. In the first pattern, after the person recovers from an injury, he or she wants to make up for lost time and overdoes it right away; too often, the result is re-injury. In the second pattern, fear about restarting causes the person not to get back as quickly as possible. If an injury, illness, or just life, has prevented you from doing much of anything for an extended length of time, it is very important to go very slowly with any increase in volume or intensity.

When I am injured, I evaluate each situation for myself. First, what got me here? If I created my own injury by increasing my volume or intensity too quickly, I need to come back more slowly. The important thing here is to look back and to listen to the present. Listening to myself can be difficult when ego and denial get in the way. I must be as honest as possible with myself to get a true picture. This is a process that can take time. Be patient and the rewards will be there if you wait for them and keep moving forward consciously. My orthopedic surgeon, who is also an athlete, says to let pain be my guide. For example, if pain is an issue, back off or stop till you can continue without pain. Listening to my coach who has probably experienced the same or similar injuries is also invaluable. In addition, a trusted online community, health professionals, and physical therapists are good resources. Listening to other people with similar injuries and learning what solutions they employed can be helpful. I don't have to re-invent the wheel every time; others have been down this road ahead of me.

Starting up again can be done cautiously by testing and waiting for your body to respond. As with increasing your intensity or training volume, listening will pay great dividends here. During the buildup to your pre-injury workloads, continue the regimen of rest, icing, compression, and elevation as needed, decreasing the therapy gradually. When I look back with a new perspective, I can see what I have gone through and learned.

CHAPTER WISDOM

Prevention is the first policy toward injuries. If they occur, then apply RICE, learn from the event, and move forward with changed expectations.

CHAPTER 20

TRAINING III: REEVALUATING THE PLAN

Suffering through an injury and the process of healing will result in changed expectations. However, you can't rush the process. Spending a lot of emotional energy trying to figure out something that is impossible to predict wastes valuable energy. So I take it one day at a time, telling myself that the whole situation will work itself out.

The knee injury I suffered leading up to the Olympic trials of 2009 gives an example of how I deal with such a situation.

I tore the meniscus cartilage of my left knee while playing tennis in 2001. I had it trimmed out surgically, and after a few weeks, I was back doing my normal activities, playing tennis, running, etc. In the spring of 2009, I re-injured my left knee. After staying away from activities that aggravated it and taking about five weeks off, I started training again.

Assuming that the rest had healed the tenderness in my left knee, I started training with too much exuberance. I did some bounding (explosive alternating, one-leg hops) on a crushed limestone trail and I landed a little crooked and felt pain in my left knee again. I finished the workout with some pain but told myself that I had worked it out before, so I could probably work it out again. I was hoping it would subside. I could still run, do low work (simulate skating on dry land), bike, lift weights, and do slide board. The only thing I couldn't do was jump.

This went on for another month until I could no longer climb stairs, lift weights, or do slide board or low work without pain. I could do only decreased-intensity biking. My orthopedic surgeon confirmed the fact I had been trying to ignore. The meniscus was torn and needed trimming again. I had to go through what I most dreaded—not the surgery, but taking time off training in an Olympic year. Accepting that fact was going to be hard. However, accepting it did not mean I had to like it.

I decided to analyze why I had denied the injury and what my behavior might mean. I realized I was angry that it was my fault for tearing up my own cartilage and jeopardizing my plans and goals. As a result, I had bargained as long as I could, compensating by getting some training done rather than none at all. I grew depressed, worrying about the down time, the lost training, and my uncertain future. Finally, I accepted reality and went to the doctor. I came to trust that this had happened for a reason. The result was a shift in my thinking. I believed there was a higher purpose to what was happening to me. It was up to me to learn from it, change my response from denial to acceptance, move forward, and make adjustments.

After the medical procedure, I rested for about a month of light or no training. The result was that I gave my body a much-needed break. Afterward, I came back with a new attitude, more enthusiasm, and a higher capacity than ever before. I had found my deeper reason. I now had the perspective of a little time away, and I was better off after having the surgery and the rest.

During the time it took to diagnose the injury and have surgery, I was able to do some physical activity. Physical activity has always had a calming effect on me, so I did things that would not exacerbate my injury. I was able to swim, bike lightly, etc. If it did not hurt, it was ok to do. I used continuous movement to help minimize the down time and speed the healing process.

Another form of injury, overtraining, has often affected my training and racing. For example, I had been working with Dave Cruikshank as my coach since the spring of 2005. During the 2010-2011 season, Dave would not be coaching, so I decided not to have a coach for a while. I had a pretty good sense of where I was and wanted to change some of the emphases in my training program. I felt I needed more strength for the high speed turns. I changed my early season off-ice work to do weight training three times per week.

When I started skating in the middle of September, I felt pretty good, maybe a little tired from flying a lot and training. Unfortunately, I was not sleeping very well or getting the rest I needed. The first major race of the season was the fall World Cup trials to be held in the middle of October in Milwaukee. I raced a couple of weekend time trials leading up to this competition, but I didn't taper off my training, so I was tired when the competition started. In fact, the prior weekend I had been so tired that my racing was not very good. I was running out of gas.

In the fall World Cup trials, I skated the 500 the first day and was totally wiped out. It seemed that I was going slower with every workout and race. After getting off the ice, I scratched skating the 1000 that I was scheduled to race an hour later. I spoke with an old friend, Nancy Swider-Peltz, Sr. (who was not yet my coach), about what was going on. She called me later and asked if I was going to skate the 1500 the next day. I said no. I realized I needed some time off from training, and I took two weeks off and did nothing but put my legs up and watch TV.

I felt that I had been here before—specifically, when I was 19 and totally burned out after the Olympic trials. I had that deep-down fatigue in my legs. The ache in my legs would not go away after a few days' rest. Two weeks stretched into four weeks. I had never taken this kind of time off in the middle of a season before, but it was necessary. When I was 19, my body took eighteen months to recover. Hoping that it would not take that long this time, I sat in front of the TV with my legs up for five weeks before doing much of anything.

Resting is hard for me, but I have learned how to do it for my own survival. I started sleeping better. Ironically, my flying assignments basically stopped. I had a couple of vacations assigned to me. Maripat and I stayed home, and I recuperated.

After five weeks, I started skating again. This time, I thought it was going to be different. I tried to start up where I left off, but that lasted only a week. I talked to Dave, my former coach, and Nancy, my friend, about what was going on, and among the three of us we figured out what to do.

First, I was just going to try to recover. I had to scale back my expectations about the rest of the season—that was the first priority. I decided that I would maybe skate the meet in Milwaukee that I was running; I could wait to decide that later. I also decided I was definitely not going to Calgary for the World Masters All-Arounds in February, but I was thinking about maybe skating another masters competition in Salt Lake in early March.

Dave suggested riding the stationary bike everyday for an hour at very low intensity to help replace the glycogen in my muscles. By low intensity, he meant hardly even breaking a sweat. Going too hard would be counterproductive. It takes a certain amount of heartbeats to restore the glycogen that my muscles needed to function.

Then Nancy suggested a very specific workout on the ice for recovery that included some speed, but not too much, and practicing some starts at the end of each ice session. Having recent experience doing starts is critical to doing well in a race. I did not do very many— just enough to get the right feel, then stop before any fatigue buildup. When skating the longer stuff, I needed to concentrate on technique and be careful not to build fatigue. After each skating workout, I would ride the bike an hour for recovery. I skated only twice a week. The other days I just rode for recovery and did a lot of stretching for flexibility and range of motion.

I continued this training program for the rest of the season. I did race in Milwaukee in January, then again in early March in Salt Lake. To my surprise, I ended up with some pretty good results. In Milwaukee, I was second fastest of all the masters. The fastest guy was 15 years younger than me. I was national champ in the 500 and 1000 for my age group. In Salt Lake I finished the season in with my best times of the year by far and a world record in my age group for the 500-meter race.

I learned some hard lessons. I was grateful that I listened to my body, which I hadn't done when I was 19. I listened to other experts in the field. As a result, I was able to go through a very difficult year and learn a great deal. Mostly, what I learned about myself was that I could change, shift my priorities, and still achieve great things.

Stress also contributes to injuries. As I consider stress in relation to injury prevention, I ask myself, "Am I internalizing my stress so that it becomes evident through an injury?" When I carry a lot of stress, it usually goes to my back and or my neck. If I try to carry the weight of the world on my shoulders, I end up with back and neck trouble. I have to be careful how I deal with and carry stress and anger. Now I watch for telltale signs in my attitude and behavior before it becomes evident in a physical way with back and neck pain. I work at finding appropriate ways to get rid of my stress and anger before they affect me in a physical way.

Let me relate an example of how stress can cause an ongoing injury and be an impediment to rest and recovery. One of the things I was aware of when trying to qualify for the Olympic trials in 2005 were masters world records. I had learned that I could compete with anybody, at any age, in speed skating. I could also compete as a master in my age group. During my training for the 2005 trials, I realized that by qualifying for the trials, I would set my age group record for the 500-meter and 1000-meter races. I thought that qualifying and setting age-group world records at the same time would be pretty cool.

At that time, I was in the 45-49 age group. The old record was 39.45 seconds for a 500-meter race. I skated a 38.95 in the trials! I also skated a 1:15.78 1000-meter! These were clearly records and faster than any man had ever gone at my age. In fact, they were faster than any man from the next younger group (ages 40-44) had gone.

Even though I submitted my times from the Olympic trials, they did not count in the eyes of the IMSSC, the international governing body for masters speed skating. So I still had to make a record-breaking time at an IMSSC-sponsored race. The following year, the masters world all-around championships were going to be in Calgary. The all-around championships include both short- and long-distance races. For men under 70 years old, the events are 500, 1500, 3000, and 5000 meters. Since I am a sprinter, the 1000-meter is my best race, and I do pretty well at the 500. However, the 1000 was not being contested at that event. What this meant was that I would train hard for another year just to skate one race, the 500 in Calgary.

After a pretty good training year following the 2005 trials, I was on a roll as an athlete. However, my personal life had major problems. I was separated from my first wife, going through a divorce, and living in an apartment near my soon-to-be-ex wife and 14-year-old daughter.

I was skating and training pretty well, but I noticed that after a race or a really hard training effort, my heart would act up. I would get a little light-headed for a few seconds and feel tightness in my left arm. I had never had any heart trouble before. I knew that the EKGs taken for my annual FAA physicals showed an extra T wave, but I was told that it was because I was an athlete. It was always consistent year after year, and it had never caused a problem.

Because I never lost my balance when it occurred, I attributed it to being over my max capacity. I wore a heart monitor regularly, and I noticed that the threshold for these symptoms was coming down from 165 beats per minute to the 150 range.

About the middle of January 2007, I mentioned it to my coach Dave. He said to get off the ice immediately and have it checked out. I went to have a CT scan for any blockage that afternoon. On a scale of 0-400, my blockage from calcium deposits was 0. Perplexed, I made an appointment to see a cardiologist in a couple of days. After I explained to him what was going on, he recommended a nuclear stress test the next day. I was able to duplicate a little of what I was going through by running on a treadmill at the end of the test. The result showed that I had a very strong heart with no blockage.

The cardiologist did not have any conclusions, so I decided that looking at my situation in its entirety was the key. I was separated and going through a divorce, working full-time for United, training full-time for the Calgary meet, sleeping poorly, and probably not getting enough rest.

The Calgary competition would be the next month. With this

condition, how could I go to Calgary to compete? I had made the reservations for Calgary and paid for my coach to be there. Even so, we decided to back off and train easier, not push my threshold for the heart issue. I also had to change my expectations for the competition. I would go, but once I was there, would I even feel like racing? Was it worth it? I decided I would see how I felt, day by day, and go with that. Because I am by nature a planner, leaving things open-ended was really tough for me. So I traveled to Calgary and went through the motions for racing.

The competition was scheduled to start February 22, 2007, with the 500-meter and 3000-meter races. The next day would be the 1500 and then the last day would be the 5000. If I felt well enough, my plan was to skate the 500 and then skate an easy 3000 later in the day. I would race hard in the 1500 and skate the 5000 if I qualified for it. Because of time restrictions, a skater must be in the top 24 of his group to do the 5000 the last day. The 50-54 men was the largest group with about 50 competitors. The entire competition was limited to about 350 men and women.

I felt well enough to race the 500 the first day. I remember very well my on-ice warm up for the 500 at that event. My pre-race warm-up routine was going as planned. Then, when I got to point where I practice the standing starts, I fell down. I may fall once or twice a season. But there in Calgary, during the warm up of my most important race of the season, I tripped and fell flat on my face. This was a wake up call! It got my attention. I was also a little embarrassed.

Dave saw me and chuckled. I shrugged my shoulders and went back to the starting line where I had fallen and lowered to my starting position. I did much better the next time. I was not really present in the moment, so I refocused. I practiced another couple of starts to end on a good note with confidence. Then I got off the ice to rest before race time.

I had the outer lane for the start. This is not my favorite starting lane. The second inner lane turn was very tricky at such high speed. I was paired with a Norwegian. We made eye contact as we approached the starting line, and I wished him good luck. I was very calm approaching the starting line, but when the gun goes off, watch out! I beat my pair to the first turn. Even though the distance to skate for the first outer turn is about 15 meters longer than the inner turn, I beat my pair to the crossover on the back straight as well.

I was unaccustomed to carrying so much speed into a second sharp turn, so I hesitated a little and entered late. Staying in my lane took all my strength. As I exited the turn, I drifted into the outer lane for a short distance. The officials don't mind as long as you do not interfere with the other skater, and I didn't because he was well behind me. I moved back into my lane, and skated to the finish. Rising up after the finish, I felt no heart issues. Rest had been what I needed. I let go of the result and focused on the task at hand. It was not my best race ever, but a good effort; I was proud of that.

Under the circumstances, it was the best I could do. I looked up at the scoreboard while gliding down the backstretch. I was the fastest, one second faster than my closest competitor and about a half a second faster than the record! A couple of pairs still had to skate. As I glided around the warm-up lane, my coach Dave congratulated me for a job well done.

A friend of mine—Gerrit Bos from London, Ontario, who was a competitor in the 70-74 year group—was yelling from the edge of the ice that I had broken the record! I had met Gerrit a number a years earlier in Milwaukee; he would drive there from London, Ontario, Canada, to train on the oval. He is a great competitor and a coach, so he could really appreciate what had just happened. My fellow age-group racers and fellow Americans congratulated me with a few high fives. I had accomplished what I set out to do for the year in one attempt, one race.

The experience of that 500-meter race contained so many lessons that it would take me quite some time to absorb them. In retrospect, my heart issue had been caused by cumulative stress. My own stress, no one else's but mine. I could look to my circumstances and point my finger. Or I could point at myself and admit that most of the stress had been self-created. I realized that I will always have stress and that the most important lesson to learn was how to handle the stress in my life. A lot of my anger was under the surface; it was being suppressed, so it was going to my heart and affecting its basic functions and efficiency. I started using some new tools to deal with my stress, including accepting the following four principles:

1. I cannot control anything but my own attitude and what I bring to the world outside of me.
2. I am not in charge of the results. I need to trust that I will get the results I am supposed to get.
3. I need to keep from adding to my own stress. Added stress usually comes in the form of my own expectations.
4. I need to keep my expectations as realistic as possible.

At the Calgary meet, I skated the 3000 a few hours after the 500. Since I had accomplished my goal, I decided to view the rest of the competition as a victory lap and a bonus. I had really trained only for the 500 that year. I had not raced a 3000 since 1975. I enjoyed every minute of it. I skated it at an easy pace so that I could be my best for the 1500 the next day. As it turned out, my time for the 3000 was an all-time personal best and more than seven seconds faster than my time in 1973.

The 1500 went very well. My time was just over two minutes. I had not raced too many 1500s during my career and hardly any since I began training seriously again. Even so, I knocked 15 seconds off my best time ever; that was about a half lap at this speed! I finished second in that race in my age group, behind the overall winner of the all-around. The last day was the 5000. Even though I had qualified for one of the final twenty-four spots to skate this race, I considered skipping it. Then I decided I owed it to my fellow competitors to race. Some had flown across the ocean to race and not made it to the final 5000. I had qualified and I should take the place I had earned on the starting line; skipping it would be an insult to my fellow masters.

For me, it would be 12-1/2 victory laps. I rarely do 12 laps in row in training. How could I do it in a race? I was afraid of the pain. Sprinters like me don't do long stuff like this. Going slow is against my nature, but I decided to do my best, be patient, and not go out too fast and run out of gas.

We skated the race in quads where one pair starts out first, then another pair a few seconds behind. I struggled and was almost lapped by my pair. Even so, I knocked 25 seconds off my best time ever from 1975. Indoor ice, better skates, a smarter me with better skating technique. All were factors that led to this great result.

Wow, what a competition. I flew home with a smile on my face that you could not wipe off. I shared that experience with everyone who played a part in my life. I celebrated the work, external and internal. The biggest takeaway was that I could wake up to my predicament, re-evaluate my plan, change my expectations, and still be ok, even thrive. The results were the tangible evidence.

My last example, from my brother Bart, shows how to have faith and keep moving after an injury.

Bart has had some major injuries in his career. His first major injury was a bicep tear. He was competing in the Olympic trials in Jacksonville, Florida, before the 1980 Summer Games. About halfway through the competition, he tore his bicep. He knew he could do his routines if he took out the more difficult skills, so he finished the meet with watered-down routines and still won the competition by a nice margin.

This was his second Olympic team. Unfortunately, before the trials, President Carter had decided that the United States would not participate in the1980 Summer Games in Moscow. Although that decision was disappointing, it did give Bart time to take care of his injury. After the meet, he went to see his orthopedic surgeon and had his bicep reattached. Bart was back in the gym six months after surgery and rehab.

In December 1983, prior to the 1984 Summer Olympic Games to

be held in Los Angeles, Bart was again at the top of his field. He was in Japan competing in the Chunichi Cup, an important international competition leading up to the Olympic Games. All the internationally renowned judges were there. Bart was in the middle of the competition on the still rings. He swung up to a handstand. He felt a familiar rip and the pop that went with it; this time he had torn the other bicep. He immediately let go of the rings and dropped to the mat on his feet. He raised his non-injured arm to the judges signifying that he had dismounted and was done. The score no longer mattered.

The next day he was on a plane headed for Salt Lake City to have his bicep reattached. This time he did not have six months to get back in the gym; he had six months till the next Olympic trials.

Bart would have been a medal contender in 1980, but he lost his chance due to global politics. Now he was 26, and his peak performances were at hand. If he made the team for 1984, he would be the oldest member. After years of the pounding abuse that gymnastics caused, his body had suffered numerous bone chips in elbows, knees, ankles, spine, etc. Bone chips in his elbow kept him from fully extending his arm. This slight bend put extra strain on his bicep, hence the tear. So he needed to have those chips in his elbow cleaned out in addition to having the bicep reattached.

Bart came out of the operating room hooked to a machine that kept his arm bending at the elbow. Mobility was the key in rehab. Medicine had advanced to the degree that new techniques for surgery and rehab were better than ever. He could be back in the gym in six weeks this time. Besides, he was very motivated—a characteristic of our family.

Training progressed as fast as he could go based on his recovery. They had to figure out what Bart needed to do just to make the team. The trials would be about six weeks before the Games in Los Angeles, so Bart would have another six weeks to train and recover after the trials. Hopefully, this would enable him to reach his peak at the Games. The first goal was just to make the team.

Bart petitioned the U.S. Gymnastics federation to allow him to bypass all the preliminary competitions to the trials because of his injury. They agreed. His first competitive routine since the last bicep tear would be in the trials.

At the trials, Bart managed to finish in sixth place. The top six places would be Olympians. The seventh place was an alternate, in case someone got hurt. Now he would have six more weeks before the Games to continue his recovery. He managed to peak at the Games. At age 26, Bart was the oldest member of the team and its leader. The men won the team championship, upsetting the dominant world champion Chinese. Bart won a gold medal for the team victory. In the individual competition, he became the first man ever to score a perfect 10. He achieved that on the parallel bars, winning another gold medal. It was his last competitive routine—a nice way to finish a career.

Bart says that he had a great career up to the point of his last injury. The two gold medals were not necessary for his career to be complete. He changed his expectations, kept moving, and had gratitude for each step along the way.

CHAPTER WISDOM

By continually reevaluating our plans and adapting to changed circumstances, we can uncover new ways to enjoy the journey and achieve our goals.

CHAPTER 21
COMPETITION

"We improve ourselves by victories over ourselves. There must be contests, and we must win." Edward Gibbon

In my teens, my self-concept and self-worth were all about my sports performance. I thought that pouring everything, all my energy, into my sport and achievement would bolster my self-esteem. I could have gone a number of directions—sports or academics—but sports and physical activity feed me. Focused and driven to the extreme, I could not be stopped from going overboard when I was young. By stepping away for a very long time, I could gain a better perspective.

Drawn back to the sport from pure love for it, I realized how much I enjoyed the training, the process, the people, everything. This time, I decided to be careful not to pick up my old ways of thinking about skating, training, and competing. Repeating past patterns could not be an option. Remaining in good shape and skating once a week for a few years was how I started my return. Putting a toe in the water and returning gradually was my path back to skating.

I kept watching out for signs of my old ways of thinking. Extreme thinking has a way of creeping back if I am not on guard. Once I was back in the sport at a high level of effort, would I travel down the same road as a teenager and encounter the same land mines?

With that in mind, I asked myself some tough questions as I re-started this process. Was I doing this to fulfill an unrealized need to achieve? How was my achievement tied to my self-worth? Was it all about the performance? Even though I had a good, balanced self-esteem in many other parts of my life, was I trying to fill this empty hole again? Would others love me if I win? Would I accept and love myself? Even though I was fearful of some of the answers, I had to know, so I kept digging. The result was that I struck gold, my gold.

Through competition, I discovered the real me. I am learning to appreciate myself more now than ever, both the good and bad. By finding things that feed me, that drive me, and that push me around—and by embracing all of them—I can be worthy of love without defining achievements. I gradually realized that my family, my loved ones, and God will love me for who I am, good and bad, not what I do or accomplish. It took me a long time to accept that. I had to work it out on my own terms, in my own time frame, to dig and find my own treasure of self-acceptance.

Part of this process of discovery was learning my love of competition. When I take out as many variables as possible, measuring my own progress against myself, competition is available to me everyday. The best person to compete with is myself.

This new way of looking at competition can be good and bad. When competition with myself is carried to an extreme, I risk running myself into the ground as I did as a teenager. Even as an adult, I can lose my sense of priorities and harm other parts of my life. Competition and achievement can become too much. By recognizing the slippery slope, I can change my path back to balance and conscious decisions. By balancing priorities, I can enjoy competing with others and myself just for the joy of it. Competition will help me uncover hidden motives that lie buried in my subconscious. When approaching the starting line, I bring all of me, whether I like it or not. This is a hard process, but it is worth the work.

Expectations are one of the land mines of competition. I spend a great deal of time training and very little time actually racing, probably a 99-to-1 ratio. Based on training volume, I should have very high expectations of my performance. After all this work, I think I should achieve great results. Expectations lead us to get ahead of ourselves. When my ego is firmly in control, I cannot live in the moment or be grateful. As a sprinter, my skating is very technical. It requires great concentration and focus. I have built a great big motor through my training; when I apply it to the ice efficiently, I achieve speed. Without focus, when I get ahead of myself and lose the moment, my technique suffers as well as my speed and efficiency.

Approaching the starting line, I repeat a mantra that helps me with my expectations. "I am grateful to be here and skate. I am confident that I have done the work to prepare. I will adjust as I go. I trust that I will get the results that I am supposed to get. I let go of the outcome, the expectations, and stay in the moment of each movement."

Competing with gratitude rather than expectations works. If I stay focused on what I am doing, the results will take care of themselves. By approaching the starting line with gratitude, I can be present in the moment. With practice, by listening to my body and head as I go, I will succeed at not burning out too fast. Being grateful helps me to function better and lose the fear of unmet expectations. A good emotional outlook will carry me far. A fearful emotional outlook will zap my energy quickly. I can apply this principle to everything in my life today. It will always carry me.

When it comes time to perform, I cannot change who I am or my skill level. So I commit to action as though nothing else matters at this moment. After the finish, I look at the scoreboard, grateful again for the opportunity to do what I love. When I see the results I have earned, I accept them without judgment.

I have been on a long journey to get to this state of mind. By applying this type of philosophy to almost everything in my life today, I have found great rewards. Even though I was so driven before, I finally woke up to these facts. Competition feeds me but no longer controls me.

During racing, energy management is critical. In speed skating, I must manage my physical and emotional energy. A human can do an all-out effort for a maximum of about 15 seconds. The shortest race I skate is 500 meters, which takes about 40 seconds. My best race is the 1000 meters, which lasts about 1 minute and 20 seconds. By going too hard at the wrong time or too early in the race, I burn out and run out of gas. When this happens, my technique suffers—resulting in lost efficiency and lost speed. Since the 500-meter race is so technical, I must keep focused and keep my emotions under control. I can summon my emotions towards the end of a race when I am physically tired, when I draw from deep down. For me, feeling too much emotional energy when I have fresh legs can be bad. I lose my patience and it affects my timing, and I loose my connection with the ice. As a result, I prefer to temper my emotion early, then draw on it later when it does not affect my timing.

Physical energy has a limit. My emotional energy is not so limited. I can draw from it when I need it, and it refreshes itself more quickly than my physiology will refresh my legs and body. By practicing drawing from this emotional energy during practice and some of the less important races, I have turned it into a valuable tool. I have experimented to find out what works for me.

Some athletes love confrontation; they thrive on emotional conflict to spur them on to great things. Experiment to find out what works for you. Emotional energy is pretty quickly renewable, but it takes practice. The ability to exercise this aspect of energy management is an essential tool that needs to be learned during training. I use my emotions in practice, to see how they affect me and benefit me, and how to manage them.

Stress is involved in all levels of competition. How we handle stress can strongly impact the outcome of our efforts. Stress is a normal human response because of the ancient fight or flight instinct. Our heart rates rise, body temperature goes up, our nerves become more sensitive, adrenaline rushes, blood sugar rises, etc. We are ready to go! If we think stress is bad for us, it will be. If we believe it is normal and we use it to prepare for competition, then it is good for us. The anxiety that can accompany stress is one of the negative consequences. Anxiety can cause us to tighten up and be unable to perform to the level that we have trained for. Our minds work in nanoseconds. I can tighten up in the middle of my downswing to hitting a golf ball or the wind up to hit a tennis ball.

It takes experience for all of us to learn how to handle stress and anxiety in the competitive environment. We all have to learn for ourselves what works and what does not. I have failed many times in the way I handle my anxiety. By keeping alert to my own thoughts and making adjustments, I make progress. My goal is to make stress an asset and keep the anxiety to a minimum.

Practicing thought processes during my training sessions helps prepare me for racing. Visualization creates confidence in the plan, in its execution, and ultimately in myself. Thoughts are self-fulfilling prophecies. We create environments that make it more likely to succeed or fail. Positive reinforcing statements that we repeat to ourselves help us to set up our minds for positive outcomes.

Nothing can substitute for the real competition. It is very important to be conscious of my thoughts before and during racing, building on what works and discarding what doesn't.

We all carry baggage into competition. Dropping the unnecessary stuff and making use of assets are the important parts of the process.

I remember one competition when I was about 15 years old that I am especially proud of—the Chicago City Championships. The rink was made by flooding a field at Waveland Park along Lake Michigan. It was the middle of January, cold and windy. The warming hut, where we huddled between heats, semifinals, and finals for all the distances, was small. A skater named Greg Berg was competing well that year, and I was watching him closely. This was a pack-style competition just like today's short track. Everyone starts together and whoever crosses the finish line first wins. I usually skated in front of the pack if possible so as to avoid getting tangled up with other skaters or blocked from moving up. The trouble with my up-front strategy was that I could be passed without much warning. As a result, I often finished in the top two or three skaters, but I rarely won. My philosophy about racing was that I would work harder than anyone else in training and then I would blow everyone away from the front. However, because the front position made it difficult to figure out what everyone was doing in the pack behind me, I had been shut out a few times. I found it unpleasant to lose just because I was in the wrong spot. That style of racing was not a true measure of who was the best skater, but rather who had the best tactics.

So I realized that if I just followed Greg and passed him at the right moment, it might work. I stuck like glue behind him until just the right time, and I passed him in every race. By using the right tactics, I won the meet. I picked the right guy to pace myself against. That time, my tactics worked. After that meet, I no longer feared tactics. Despite that success, however, I decided I still preferred time-trials racing. To me, it is the purest form of racing and the purest form of competition. My own lane, the clock, and me.

CHAPTER WISDOM
Competition can reveal our true selves and provide growth and healing.

CHAPTER 22

BALANCE AND PRIORITIES

Balance is a fine art. Using the analogy of walking on a beam is a helpful way to look at balance. When I started out on this journey, the beam was very wide. Falling off was not so painful or costly. As I have become more conscious, the beam has gotten narrower and tougher to stay upon. The rewards for staying on are much higher, and the pain of falling off is greater as well. We all fall off the beam—get out of balance—from time to time; it is part of life, and so is pain. I get back on the beam more quickly now, with less of a wound and one that heals faster. As time has passed, and I have become more sensitive to being off balance, I can stay on for longer periods of time. It is a great reward, providing a sense of peace and stability.

Balance is essential to my life, but it is easier to talk about not having balance. We all know the effect of being out of balance. Some of the consequences include being unfocused, inefficient, unproductive, exposed to injury and disease. Being in balance is just the opposite. We are focused, productive, efficient, healthy, happy, content, and serene. This is what I strive for. Making the necessary corrections to stay on the beam gets easier when we are more conscious to our state of mind. This is a learning process like anything else. The benefits are applicable to all areas of my life, and I must give balance the top priority that it deserves. Most of us spend about 90% of our time looking over the edge and trying to stay in balance. By finding out what works, continuing to do it, and refining it little by little, I make progress.

Priorities are the foundation of good decision-making. By keeping my priorities straight, I can make good judgments about where I am, where I want to go, and how to get there. If I am confused about my decisions, revisiting my priorities will help my decisions become clearer. God first, family second, work third, recreation fourth—those are my guidelines.

I know a few people who are very busy but always seem to have time for the most important things. This is an example of having priorities straight. There is an old saying that states, "Anything that is urgent is rarely important, and anything that is important is rarely urgent." Sometimes the best ideas are also the simplest.

I am much calmer now than I was in previous years. I have found it is easier with time to live lighter and even more passionately. This has been a continual growth process for me. My self-esteem used to be tied to my achievements, so until I accomplished all that I could, I could not rest. Striving for better balance helps me remember my priorities and keep them straight.

Conflicts are a part of life and inevitable. Some are more important than others, so prioritizing is necessary. One thing I try to remember to ask is, "How important is it really? Will I remember this issue a few days from now, a few weeks from now?" The answers will usually tell me how to handle the situation. If someone cuts me off in traffic, what do I do? I can make a choice if I put on the pause button. After pausing, reviewing, and prioritizing, then I can determine how important it is. By playing out the conflict and seeing the possible outcomes, I can get a clearer vision. Usually most conflicts are not about me; the situation will usually solve itself with no intervention by me at all. This is a much easier way to live. When a response is required, then I can choose how to proceed.

Back to getting cut off in traffic, I need to protect myself first. Then I can choose what to do next. Most of the time, I choose to do nothing. If I hang onto the conflict with the person who has cut me off, then I have chosen to carry the conflict now. The other driver may not even be aware of cutting me off, so why should I carry on the conflict? I can choose what do with the situation. I can feel the feelings and then let them go, or I can hang onto them and poison myself.

Anger happens. It is a normal human emotion. I used to fear my anger. Now I can see it for what it is, normal. I used to be afraid of the actions that I carried out after being angry. I can separate the two now.

My anger comes from fear. Anger helps keep me separated from my fears and keeps them at arm's length. Fear can keep me safe, but it can also push me around if I give it power over me. If I hang onto the fear, it can turn to anger and I might do something I would regret. Now I can handle fear and its resultant anger better by letting it go and putting things in their proper place.

Stress is also a normal condition. My stress level is usually contingent on my mental state. If I am doing well, I can handle a great deal of stress. If I am not doing well, just a little extra can seem to push me over the edge. I continually deal with stress in my life. I can give it power, or I can let it rule me. It is my choice. I need to develop and practice how to handle stress. I won't be very good at it until I have been successful at handling some easy situations first. Then with some experience, I can handle tougher situations.

Traffic is usually a pretty good barometer of how I am handling the stress in my life. If I have a short fuse and everyone seems to be driving poorly around me, then I must look at myself to see where I am. Am I overly sensitive about my surroundings and threatened at every turn? By looking at how I am handling my stress, I can expose the underlying problems in my life. It is not the traffic that is the problem but how I respond to the traffic. That is the mirror I need to look at to see what is really going on with me. As I continually learn and grow, my answers change with time.

Stress is a normal part of everyday life. Stress is either self-created, on purpose, or it is created outside of me and I must choose a response to it. The stress that I feel before a race is my creation; I choose to race. It can be frightening and rewarding just the same. I have control over this stress. It's the stress that I have no control over that drives me nuts.

After I recognize my stress level, what do I do with it? Usually my stress comes out in anger. Sometimes I bury it and it affects me physically by making me sick (dis-ease). By learning how to deal with my anger, I can manage my stress. Physical activity helps with my anger. Going for a long run, chopping down a tree, doing yoga, and meditating are examples of physical things I can do to facilitate healing. That is probably why I train so hard. It is a productive and healthy way to deal with my stress. I have also learned to defuse my anger slowly instead of going from zero to rage. Using my networks of support and getting help for my mental and emotional state works for me. Knowing I am not alone in my struggles helps as well. After building confidence in my ability to handle my stress, I can deal with anything that comes my way.

It takes experience for each of us to learn how to handle stress and anxiety. We all have to learn for ourselves what works and what does not. I have failed many times in the way I handle my anxiety. By keeping alert to my own thoughts and making adjustments, I make progress.

A lower stress level helps me to rest better, feel healthier, recover faster, and train harder. Sometimes I just need to take the lead from my dog: let go, run and play, be happy.

To balance on a skate blade, I must be right physically. I must have strength, endurance, and the heart and lungs to provide my muscles with the proper nutrients and oxygen. I must be mentally focused when hurtling around a 25-meter radius corner at 35 miles per hour. I must be emotionally available to dig deep for strength. I must be spiritually fit to trust that I am in the right place in the universe at this moment. Skating provides me with tangible immediate feedback about the state of my physical, mental, emotional, and spiritual balance.

CHAPTER WISDOM

Balance is a great barometer for all parts of my life, both internal and external.

CHAPTER 23

MENTAL SUPPORT

Most of the concepts in this book are grounded in thinking. Everything starts with a thought. Paying attention to mental health and well-being is critical. You cannot heal a sick mind with a sick mind. If I am isolated with my own thoughts, not sharing what is down deep or what is going on in my mind, I will develop some very sick thinking. Getting thoughts out into the light of day is difficult and scary. By seeing my thoughts in a mirror, I can start to evaluate and decide what to change. The steps are letting go of what is bad, emphasizing what is good, and then beginning the healing process. All of us are sick to a degree. We are as sick as our secrets. When I share my deepest thoughts with someone I can trust, I realize I am not so different and my problems are not so bad. Being willing to share will start the process of improving my mental health, and break down the first barrier to denial.

I have other people in my life who share my path. This helps me feel not so strange or alone, and it is very comforting and healing. In many areas of my life, I share a path with others like me. Self-reliance was what I valued growing up. This concept helped me to forge my own way, to be accountable and responsible to myself. My self-esteem was built upon my own free will and was reflected by my accomplishments. It made me feel unique in the world.

However, when I saw only the differences, the world was a very cold and lonely place. Now that I look for the similarities, the world is an inviting, open, and all-inclusive place that helps and supports me. When I was young, asking for help made me think I was weak. I had to learn that great men of courage ask for help. Humility helps me find my rightful place in the universe. I find help, support, and similarities in many areas of my life today if I look for them.

My goal is to separate my life into different parts and seek out groups that can help me find solutions to my problems. It is not possible to find one person or one group that can provide support in all areas of life. Rather, I need many different support groups and people to support the many areas of my life.

When I am honest about my problems, I can seek solutions from people who have had similar issues. I do not need to reinvent the wheel everyday. I can tap into great resources this way. The people I turn to don't have to know it all; they can help me even if they are just a little farther along the road.

If all I can draw upon is my own education, background, and experience, my possible solutions to any problem are finite. By tapping into a group, I have much greater base for solutions. God speaks to me in a number of ways. One way is through other people. Another way is through inspiration. If I am open to it, solutions can come to me this way. Sometimes even the innocence of a child can provide me with help, if I choose to see it. I never know what can happen, so I try to be open to all sources of inspiration for help with my mental state of health and well-being.

I believe in the value of professional therapy and have used it on occasion. An impartial professional can help me get through tough times. In therapeutic sessions, I must be as honest as possible to allow the process of working with a therapist to be effective. Honesty and hard work with a therapist will yield great results of better mental health.

I read some kind of inspirational material everyday. Sometimes I change what I read rather than stick with one thing. Reading quotations from famous people is motivational. The wisdom of simple quotes can be very powerful.

Starting my day by doing some inspirational reading, followed by some quiet time helps me to be grounded and usually leads to inspiration. Solutions to problems that have been bothering me may come if I am quiet. I love what St Francis de Sales said about meditation: "Half an hour of meditation is essential except when you are very busy.

Then a full hour is needed." It seems odd to me to put all that time into mediation, especially when I am so busy. Well, if my mind, and body are really busy, then I need more time to meditate so that I can move forward in a centered way. If I am scattered, I will not be very efficient in my thinking or my actions. That usually leads to doing things over again.

I am grateful to have found and put into action this kind of environment in my home today. Maripat and I share our tools for our mental health and well-being. We read together each morning to start our day, then I go off to meditate for a few minutes on my own, as does she.

Yoga can also help with a number of issues. First, the stretching of the body helps me feel better physically. Yoga has a multitude of physical benefits such as power, strength, flexibility, and endurance. Feeling better physically helps me feel better emotionally. It is a great circle to be in. In addition, the mindfulness of yoga can help me feel centered. Mental balance and centeredness are great byproducts that keep me coming back for more.

I have found a relationship with a God of my understanding. Being a flawed human being who needs constant vigilance, I am not capable of healing myself. I need to bring in something greater than me to change my thinking. God can do that for me. He can help interrupt my thought process so I can change my direction, then learn and grow into the person he created me to be. I find great comfort in this philosophy. Knowing that I am never alone in this world is very comforting. I now understand that I am in exactly the place I am supposed to be in at this moment. Acceptance is the key.

Being part of a group is very important. As I mentioned before, I have a group of men whom I call my brothers, who have gone before me in this process of getting better mentally. Drawing on their strength, wisdom, hope, and leadership helps me to pass on to others the same tools and experiences that I have learned. This process strengthens my own sense of self-worth and value.

One of the tools I learned was to make a list of the things I felt deprived of as a child. This is a list of what I felt, not necessarily what really happened. For example, my father may have loved me very dearly, yet I may not have been able to understand the way he expressed himself to me. So I may have been loved but not able to really feel that love. It is my interpretation and feelings that are important in this exercise.

After I made my list, I shared it with a trusted friend. He shoved the list right back at me and said that it named my most important moral values. This was what I was striving for in my life! That assertion shocked me! How could this be? After further discussion, I understood that what I felt deprived of was what drove me.

When I started looking at my thought life and the motives behind my thoughts and actions, that analysis started revealing some very deep issues to work through. Once I figured out what really drives me, I needed to figure out my wants and needs. Making a list of wants and needs and putting it on paper sent a message to the universe. First I started to own my needs and wants, and I began to feel like I deserved to have those things. If I was willing to do the work, I could have my wants and needs met. This continues to be an evolving process for me.

Believing that I was worth it was a stretch for me at times. I had to learn that if I am to be of service to others, I must take care of myself first. The analogy of caring for a sick loved one is helpful here. If I place all my energy into the care of another to the point of sacrificing my own needs, after a while I become bitter and resentful. Eventually, I break down to the point that I am no longer able to help anyone else, even myself.

What would people think if they really knew what was going on in my head? After sharing what I was thinking with some trusted friends and therapists, I realized that I was not so different from everyone else. Most people think and want the same things. I am unique, but people have more similarities than differences.

Once I created a list of wants and needs—thus naming and claiming them—I had a better chance of them coming to fruition in my life. A journey of a thousand miles begins with the first step. I had begun to take my first steps. My list of needs and wants included a desire to share my life with someone who shares my way of thinking. As I have explained before, I was asked a question by a psychiatrist a few years ago that was very revealing. He asked me if during my first marriage we had a unity candle. I remembered that during the ceremony, the priest a lit candle. He passed the flame to both of us. We then used our separate candles to light the unity candle together. This symbolized the union of our two flames. We then blew out our individual candles. In essence, I poured all I had into the marriage for the sake of the marriage. I blew out my own identity for the sake of the marriage. Once I realized that I had lost my identity, I set about reclaiming it.

I believe that we have more power within ourselves than we realize. I am more interested in breaking down barriers than anything else. Everything starts with a thought, then is followed by action, which usually reinforces the thought and so forth. I have control over my thoughts and actions. They support each other. I am a physical manifestation of what I think. I can choose an unlimited upward spiral or a downward self-defeating one. It is purely my choice, my responsibility, my reward.

CHAPTER WISDOM

Honest, mindful attention to my thinking will guide me through all of my internal and external activities toward wholeness.

PART THREE

CHAPTER 24

COURAGE

As I mentioned at the beginning of this book, the Chinese symbol for courage has two parts. The first part is the sign for danger; the second part is opportunity. Faced with danger, I have a choice. Running from danger is sometimes the smart choice. However, facing danger can be an opportunity for growth, resulting in transformation.

Another definition for courage is "fear that has said its prayers." Trusting that things will turn out the way they are supposed to gives me the courage to go forward in a conscious way and have the attitude that the results will be perfect. I believe in doing the best that I can because quitting is not in my nature. This attitude will yield the best results even though they may not be what I was hoping for. Stress and challenge, mixed with some courage, will usually tell me what I am really made of.

My father gave me a book recently to read as I was writing this manuscript. The book, *The Adversity Quotient* by Paul Stolz, talks about three kinds of people. When they face a hill up ahead, people react in one of three ways: the climbers, the campers, and the quitters.

Once a climber gets to the top of the hill, he or she will look for another one to climb. I am a climber. Campers are people that climb only so far. They decide that the view up there is good enough, so they camp on the side of the hill. The problem with campers is that they start sliding backwards and do not even notice it. Pretty soon they are at the bottom of the hill again, wondering how they got there. Life is never still. We are always moving, forward or backward. Quitters cannot seem to climb very far before they decide that the climb is not worth the effort and just turn around.

Which are you? We all have choices; we can each choose to be a climber if we want to. Climbing is a learned activity for anyone. Make sure that you also look up and enjoy the view sometimes. Climbing is such a joy for me that sometimes I forget to look around and appreciate the view. It takes courage to climb, but the rewards are pretty cool.

Turning negative illusions into positive truths is what I strive for. My story and the philosophy I live is an example of courage. People tell me I have an inspirational story. If I could boil that story down into one piece of advice, it would be that finding the courage deep within you to break down your barriers is the key to making a better life.

Practicing Gratitude

Understanding the need to practice gratitude has been a gradual byproduct of my journey. Once I lost my sense of entitlement, I gained a new sense of wonder. A few years ago I crashed emotionally. My self-esteem was tied up in what I did for a living. I let my career and other people define me. That was my fault.

I had a very narrow view of myself when that happened. Over time, however, I found that I was much more than what I did or accomplished. After a while, I was able to appreciate what I did have. A shift in attitude was necessary. With my external identity gone, I needed to build my self-esteem from the inside, so I started out on my inward journey. It turned out I was much more than my job or accomplishments. Zen philosophy says that we should expect nothing in this world. Therefore, anything we have is a bonus. I do not subscribe to this totally. However, I do believe that gratitude helps me set the stage for good things to happen. When I actively practice gratitude, it affects everything in my life.

Seeing all the miracles around me in the lives of others helps me to reinforce this concept of gratitude. Is gratitude is a miracle magnet? I find that when I keep myself in a place of gratitude, then I tend to see and be a part of more miracles. It is an upward spiral that I choose to ride on by merely changing my attitude and outlook. It works in my life, and I have found it to be pretty powerful stuff.

PART THREE

Andrew Love, a prominent U.S. masters skater living in Salt Lake, brought the Masters World Sprint Championships to Milwaukee in February of 2009. He called upon me, as a prominent local masters skater, to help with preparations for the competition. It was an honor. Andrew would be the meet leader and would need help with the local details of the event. Olu Sijuwade, another local mainstay in Milwaukee masters community, would be the registrar. I would be responsible for the local events by organizing the Friday evening draw, food for that event, the closing banquet on Sunday, and the awards ceremony at the conclusion.

This meet created a lot of distractions from my training. I was constantly on the phone and sending e-mails to all the parties involved in the event. In retrospect, everything went very well. Despite the distractions, I was pleased with my performance. In addition, I won the 50-54 age group and also clocked the second fastest time in the competition among all the age groups. Andrew beat me, but then again, he is 15 years younger than me.

An unexpected benefit happened on Sunday. Andrew and I took turns announcing the awards and handing out the trophies and medals. As a youngster, I always had the greatest respect for the Dutch skaters. Their culture is built around skating. It is practically their national sport, and they respect the ice and all who can fly on it. After the awards were over, the Dutch masters skaters approached me for my photo and autograph! I was glad to take photos and sign the race results with my friends and competitors. Later, my father pointed out to me the significance of what had happened because I did not recognize it at the time. The Dutch had been honoring me! Through my racing and involvement with the meet, I had earned their respect. They were expressing it to me by asking for pictures and autographs to remember me by.

It still blows me away that what I did can be held in such high regard. To think that what I love to do has such an impact on others humbles me. Here is proof, and I had to be told it was there for me. A deep sense of being on the right track was an unexpected result of all this work. Other results included validation for the work—external and internal—and a sense of peace and contentment. Seeing others do something inspiring is a catalyst for all of us.

Special Needs

When I think about people with special needs, I automatically think that things are different for them. But they are really not very different at all. I know a few people that have some special needs. Some of them have needs that are physical, some mental. We all have some special needs. Being told at age 16 that I would never fly for a living because I wore glasses was a handicap I chose not to acknowledge. I know that for most people, it is not that easy to ignore their special needs. Some people have very real mental and physical barriers. Even so, the philosophies I have been talking about in this book can apply to them as well. When people with significant mental and physical barriers decide to pursue a sport, they need to set up realistic expectations and goals. Setting up a network for support is probably the most important thing to do. Getting their physical, mental, emotional, and spiritual needs met is essential. For some of these athletes, even the simple task of getting to practice facilities or competitions requires a network. The principles of networking I explained earlier are the same, just applied a little differently so that more basic needs are met first before going onto higher plateaus.

I am reminded of a very dear friend who has multiple sclerosis. His MS can make it very difficult to exercise in any kind of heat. He was a speed skater before he was diagnosed. Since the indoor rink where we skate is usually about 50 degrees, he can function pretty well in that environment and get some exercise to stimulate his muscles and nerves. However, to do this, he had to figure out how to get onto the rink. He used to walk with a cane to the edge of the rink. Then he put on his speed skates, pushed off, and glided away. Now he does not use a cane when he walks and is skating better than a few years ago. He has set up a network of support so that he can do what he loves as well as get the benefit of the environment of the cool air inside the rink. For safety, he stays out of the fast race lanes and skates in the slower lane where he can go at his own pace.

My friend's expectations of going fast are relative. His expectations are very different than mine or anyone else's. He is simply happy when he skates, and the fact that he is slowly getting faster is proof that the joy in the effort makes it all worthwhile.

I have wondered what my life would be like if I could not do the physical things that help keep me sane, healthy, and balanced today. I believe I would be confident to switch gears and go another direction, such as turning right at the next corner. It would be hard, but I would do it. The process is much the same.

During the writing of this book over the last four years, I have changed and evolved. I have remarried. My new wife Maripat has had some physical challenges as well. While skiing on January 1, 2012, she fell and got the trifecta of ACL, MCL, a meniscus tear, and a crack in the rear of the tibial plateau in her left knee. This has put some physical barriers in our way. All of this was happening while she was fighting thyroid cancer. I can look at these circumstances now as being part of my world for a reason, and I want to learn from these issues. We continue to learn and grow together.

I hope that you have learned from my experiences and that you can relate to my insights and stories. Applying the principles that I have talked about in this book can be very rewarding. I have a great life today, but it is by no means perfect. I struggle daily with the usual problems. By applying these life principles and doing the necessary work, I have a new peace. Life keeps getting better and more rewarding.

Because of my own experiences, I feel confident in saying that if you put in the work, you will reap the benefits. But it is not all about work. I am not sure of anything except that I am in exactly the place I am supposed to be in. I will continue to have challenges, obstacles, and new barriers. I continue walking through life consciously and using the tools that have served me well. Trust and faith have guided me through past success. Not only will I be OK, but I can and will thrive regardless of my circumstances. You can find what I have come to know. Break down your barriers and write your own story of successful living.

CHAPTER WISDOM

Take the risk, keep moving with courage, and practice gratitude for the journey toward wholeness.

PART THREE

RECORD TIMES

Here are some of my performance statistics for a comparison over the years.

Personal best times up to 12/31/1975

500 Meters	41.82	12/21/1975	Milwaukee, WI
1000 Meters	1:26.65	12/27/1975	Milwaukee, WI
1500 Meters	2:16.0	11/11/1975	Groningen, Holland
3000 Meters	4:59.0	12/28/1973	Milwaukee, WI
5000 Meters	8:49.2	12/29/1973	Milwaukee, WI

All long track skating before 1988 was done outdoor and was therefore subject to temperature extremes, wind, and varying ice conditions.

All of my personal best times listed below were on indoor rinks.

Personal Best Times as of this Writing:

500 Meters	38.47	3/20/2009	Salt Lake, UT, USA
1000 Meters	1:15.78	12/27/2005	Salt Lake, UT, USA
1500 Meters	1:59.41	3/21/2009	Salt Lake, UT, USA
3000 Meters	4:51.97	2/22/2007	Calgary, AB, CANADA
5000 Meters	8:25.22	2/24/2007	Calgary, AB, CANADA

These recent times are verifiable from www.speedskatingresults.com

APPENDIX

Masters World Records Men 50-54 age group

500 Meters	39.05	2/22/2007	Calgary, AB, CA
500 Meters	39.04	1/10/2009	Milwaukee, WI, USA
1000 Meters	1:17.92	1/10/2009	Milwaukee, WI, USA (since broken)
Sprint Somalog	156.670	1/11/2009	Milwaukee, WI, USA (since broken)

(combination of 500m x2 and 1000m x2)

Masters World Records Men 55-59 age group

500 Meters	38.75	3/16/2013	Salt Lake, UT, USA
1000 Meters	1:16.46	3/16/2013	Salt Lake, UT, USA
1000 Meters	1:16.15	3/17/2013	Salt Lake, UT, USA
Sprint Somalog	154.215	3/17/2013	Salt Lake, UT, USA

The record keepers of masters categories records are done by the International Masters Speed Skating Committee. The requirement for recognition as a masters record is that the race must be executed in an approved masters competition with 5-year age groups. See www.IMSSC.org for verification. Data from a particular masters season that extends from October through March is not updated usually till the following October. For example, for the just-completed 2013-2014 season, records will be updated October 2014.

The Sprint somalog above is defined as the total points accumulated from a two-day competition covering 500-meter and 1000-meter first day plus 500-meter and 1000-meter second day.

As a comparison of speed skating times from slower to faster, you can use a distance formula. When I am at top speed in the 500-meter or 1000-meter races, I am traveling at about 13 to 14 meters per second. The longer races are a bit slower. Translated into distance, this would mean if I am 1 second faster in the 500-meter race, that would be about 13 to 14 meters or 35 to 40 feet ahead of myself at the finish line.

Website

www.brucewconner.com

Blog

www.fasterasamaster.wordpress.com

Contact Bruce through his website contact form at www.brucewconner.com

Links to videos of Bruce Skating and news stories on You Tube

youtu.be/ZBZzUPqvviQ   Bruce W Conner Speed Skating 500 Meter Race Milwaukee, WI 1/26/2013

youtu.be/YXlIWR6FbsE   Bruce Conner 2009 Olympic Speedskating Trials 500 m Race

youtu.be/LISiZk2oZMI   Today's TMJ4 Sports Video at age 52, Speed skater Makes His Olympics

youtu.be/pB8bwRk2sUw   Bruce Conner on the NBC Today Show

APPENDIX

CHAPTER WISDOM RECAP

1. Keep moving and be mindful, and you will put yourself into positions that will be right for you.
2. Core self-esteem is built from within and is not based on performance. Rather, it is the result of how we feel about ourselves.
3. By taking small steps every day, we exercise courage to heal our old wounds from within and to become whole.
4. We are not alone. We have the benefit of many resources, seen and unseen, to help us get past our barriers, internal and external.
5. Ask the universe for what you need. Keep moving, and trust that whatever comes your way is in your best interest.
6. By breaking down barriers, we can show ourselves and the world that we are more capable than we give ourselves credit for.
7. Keep moving in the direction of your goals, adjust as necessary to meet the present circumstances, accept what you cannot control, and trust that you are on the right path.
8. Define blocks to progress, figure out a way around them, set your goals, act, and trust the path ahead.
9. Getting better and going faster is more about intention and choices than age.
10. The support of parents and grandparents comes in many forms and can be used throughout our lives.
11. Our networks are wider than we know and can work in better ways than we can predict.
12. Spousal support is extremely helpful. Other support can come from almost anyone to whom I have spread good will.

13. By enjoying the journey as well as the finish, I use goals as my vehicle for making external and internal progress toward wholeness.
14. Recognize and deal with your ego and emotions to your advantage.
15. Being disciplined enough to bring my "A" game to everything I do sets up the best outcomes.
16. Proper nutrition sets up the body and mind to do great work. Discipline with nutrition will pay great dividends, internal and external.
17. Be coachable, and find and foster a coach-athlete relationship.
18. Build the motor and learn how to apply it to your endeavor. Utilize the principles of practice, warm-up, cool-down, volume, intensity, strength, cardio, periodization, stretching, mental training, and rest.
19. Prevention is the first policy toward injuries. If they occur, then apply RICE, learn from the event, and move forward with changed expectations.
20. By continually reevaluating our plans and adapting to changed circumstances, we can uncover new ways to enjoy the journey and achieve our goals.
21. Competition can reveal our true selves and provide growth and healing.
22. Balance is a great barometer for all parts of my life, both internal and external.
23. Honest, mindful attention to my thinking will guide me through all of my internal and external activities toward wholeness.
24. Take the risk, keep moving with courage, and practice gratitude for the journey toward wholeness.

APPENDIX

THOUGHTS ON SOCHI 2014 WINTER OLYMPIC GAMES

The results of these winter games for U.S. skaters were the worst in very long time. Typically, the U.S. team earns many medals in long track. During the 2014 Olympics, the U.S. team came away with no medals, which is very unusual. The U.S. long track skaters did the work to arrive at the games as well prepared as possible. Expectations were high due to a number of factors, including the fact that they had all skated very well up to a few weeks prior to the games. The team was winning world cup races and setting world and track records leading up to the games. Expectations were high and for good reasons due to past performance.

We all have support networks that we rely upon or are forced to work with. In the United States, the governing body is U.S. Speedskating (USS). If you are selected to be on the national team and choose to use the support, you must live and train in Salt Lake at altitude. You must also use the coaches provided to you by the organization. The Sochi Olympics were contested at sea level. There is a significant difference in skating technique used at altitude versus sea level. There is benefit to training at altitude and racing at sea level, but the advantage wears off in a few short weeks. The difficulty of skating at sea level on slower ice is more pronounced than the benefit of training at altitude.

Many members of the Olympic team trained at Milwaukee (sea level) with independent coaching and virtually no support from USS. The fall World Cup trials as well as the Olympic trials were held in Salt Lake prior to the Olympics. This favored the Salt Lake skaters to make the team and promoted training in Salt Lake, which was counterproductive to the type of ice at Sochi.

The clothing manufacturer Under Armor developed a new skin

suit but did not want to race test it for fear of losing the advantage of a jump in technology. It turned out that this skin suit had features that made it slower. By race testing this earlier, the manufacturer could have discovered and corrected the problems. Unfortunately, the negative effect of the suit (similar to pulling a parachute behind you) exhausted the skaters' legs during the first races at Sochi. None of the skaters were able to recover after switching to an older suit in time to have any good results at the Olympics. After racing in a slow suit, it takes time to recover; I think it takes about two weeks. A number of skaters competed in World Cup events two weeks following the games and were again at the top of the podium.

Another factor in the results was the requirement for the entire team, including independently coached skaters, to train at altitude on an outdoor rink in Italy three weeks before the Games. The combination of outdoor ice and cold temperatures zapped skaters' energy levels. For the Milwaukee skaters, transitioning to altitude added additional stress on the body. All these factors are similar to overtraining. Poorly planned travel times (very early) also added unnecessary stress.

The basic principles of periodization, tapering, and complete recovery before an important competition, which I outlined earlier in this book, were violated here. I do not make anything but minor changes prior to racing. That principle was also violated. It is easier to train at sea level and transition to altitude than the other way around due to the technical difference of slower ice at sea level.

Logistics must also be considered as well. After arriving at Sochi, the team did a great deal of walking, which fatigued their legs. This could have been avoided by using bikes. The second week they had bikes, but by then, it was too late for recovery. The independent coaches had been speaking up and raising questions about the violations of basic training principles but to no avail. Unfortunately, the skaters paid the price of wasting a once-in-a-lifetime opportunity to shine at the Olympics due to poor decisions by the team management of USS.

The following month, the final Speed Skating World Cup events were held in Germany and The Netherlands. The U.S. skaters who achieved so well in the fall repeated their dominance. One skater I train with, Brian Hansen, won the 1500-meter race setting a track record. He was sufficiently recovered by then to perform at the level he trained to—further proof that the decisions prior to the Olympic Games set the stage for the poor results.

BIBLIOGRAPHY FOR FURTHER READING

Anderson, Walter. *Courage Is a Three Letter Word.* New York: Random, 1986.

Bernardot, Dan. *Advanced Sports Nutrition.* Champaign, IL: Human Kinetics, 2000.

Berquist, Lee. *Second Wind.* Champaign, IL: Human Kinetics, 2009.

Gonazales, Laurence. *Deep Survival.* New York: Norton, 2003.

Hoff, Benjamin. *The Tao of Pooh.* New York: Penguin, 1982.

Karnazes, Dean. *Ultra Marathon Man.* New York: Penguin, 2006.

Maltz, Maxwell, *Psycho-Cybernetics.* New York: Prentice-Hall, 1960

McDougall, Christopher. *Born to Run.* New York: Vintage, 2011.

McGuff, Doug and John Little. *Body by Science.* New York: McGraw Hill, 2009.

Rickman, Rick and Donna Wares. *The Wonder Years.* San Francisco: Chronicle, 2009.

Stolz, Paul. *The Adversity Quotient.* New York: Wiley, 1997.

Torres, Dara with Elizabeth Weil. *Age Is Just a Number.* New York: Broadway, 2009.

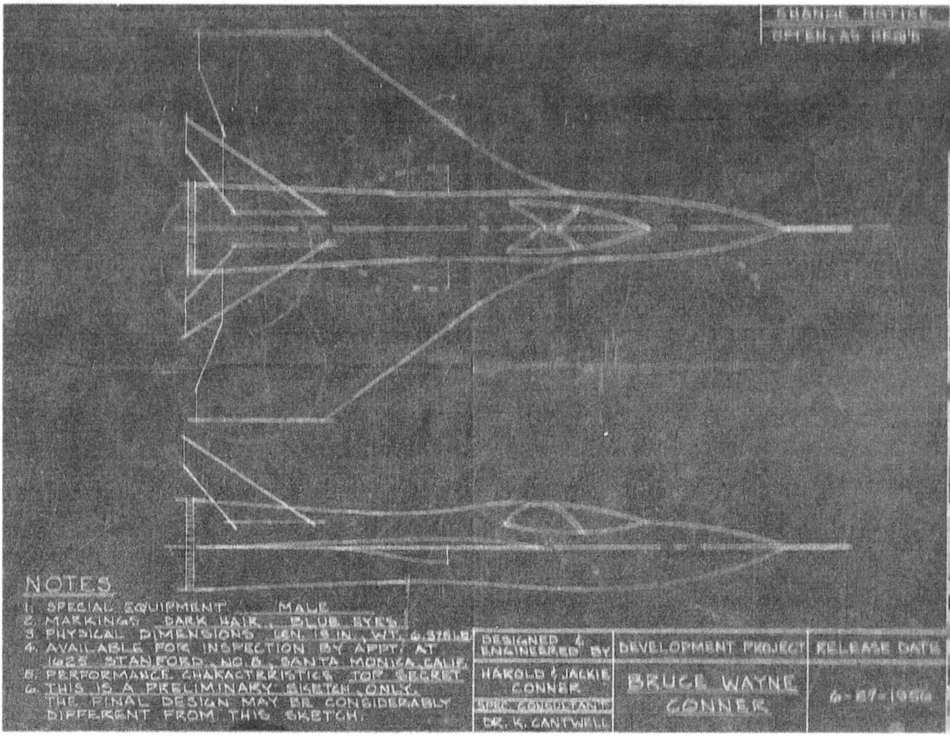

Birth Announcement Blueprint by Harold Conner

Salt Lake City, UT World Masters Sprint Championships

Bruce landing at O'hare after flight from Hong Kong, China.

uniform ready to fly!

Jackie Conner 1997

uce and Maripat Conner Milwaukee, WI. 2/16/2008

Three Conner Boys Bruce (8), Bart, (6), Michael (3) 1964t

Bruce racing in Milwaukee, WI 1970

Bruce racing in Milwaukee, WI 1972   *Bruce racing in Milwaukee, WI 1974*

Harold Conner in 747 cockpit with Bruce before departure Chicago to London August 2011

Training group in Milwaukee October 2013 Jeffrey Swider-Peltz, Nancy Swider-Peltz, Jr, Brian Hansen, Maripat Conner, Bruce Conner, Nancy Swider-Peltz, Sr.

Bart's wedding to Nadia in Bucharest, Romania

Nancy Swider-Pletz, Sr, Bruce and Brian Hansen, US Olympic trials 2014

Victor Van Den Hoff and Bruce Conner, Inzell Germany, 2/15/2009 5000m finish (final race of this competition).

www.ingramcontent.com/pod-product-compliance
Lightning Source LLC
Chambersburg PA
CBHW061639040426
42446CB00010B/1491